D0616247

In the Company of the Wise

OTHER BOOKS BY THE AUTHOR

Kundalini: Yoga for the West

Hatha Yoga: The Hidden Language

Seeds of Light

The Divine Light Invocation

Mantras: Words of Power

Radha: Diary of a Woman's Search

The Hatha Yoga Workbook

VIDEOS BY THE AUTHOR

Demons and Dragons

Hatha Yoga: The Hidden Language of the Body

The Wheel of Life

In the Company of the Wise

Remembering My Teachers, Reflecting The Light

Swami Sivananda Radha

Timeless Books

publishers of timeless wisdom

PO Box 50905, Palo Alto, CA 94303

1991

TIMELESS BOOKS
PO Box 50905
Palo Alto, CA 94303-0673
(415) 321-8311

In Canada: Timeless Books, Box 9, Kootenay Bay, B.C.
V0B 1X0 – (604) 227-9224

In England: Timeless Books, 7 Roper Rd., Canterbury, Kent
CT2 7EH – (0227) 768813

Some parts originally published in *Gods Who Walk the Rainbow* in 1981

Printed in the United States of America

Illustration of Sai Baba by Margaret White

Cover and interior design by Mike Yazzolino

Photographs by Swami Saradananda and Joe Gnilka

Library of Congress Cataloging-in-Publication Data:
Sivananda Radha, Swami. 1911–
In the company of the wise: remembering my teachers, reflecting the light / Swami Sivananda Radha
"Some parts originally published in Gods who walk the rainbow in 1981"—T.p. verso.
Includes bibliographical references.
ISBN 0-931454-23-9 (cloth) : $22.95
ISBN 0-932454-24-7 (paper): $14.95
1. Gurus. 2. Spiritual life (Hinduism) I. Title
BL 1241.48.S58 1991 91-7431
294.5′61—dc20 CIP

Dedicated to the gurus that I have met

Contents

Acknowledgements

I am grateful for having had an excellent team. My first collaborators and editors, Swami Padmananda, Margaret Gray, and Jim Spencer not only edited the original manuscript for *Gods Who Walk the Rainbow,* but it was due to their constant encouragement that I finally was convinced to share these most personal experiences with a wider circle of seekers. Joe Gnilka and Swami Saradananda took the many photographs included here, and Danita Holldorson spent many hours painstakingly restoring the old negatives. These photographs bring back fond memories of a life that seems to belong to another world.

For helping to reveal the new "secrets" in *In the Company of the Wise,* I have to thank Linda Anne Seville, my publisher, who showed great enthusiasm for all the new material and offered her continuing cooperation, which was always appreciated. My extremely conscientious editor and research assistant, Julie McKay, had her own great patience and insight, and an outstanding dedication to the Work. Ian MacKenzie fastidiously reviewed the final manuscript to ensure that the finer points of the English language were in place. Norman MacKenzie, always aware that I was looking for evidence, skimmed the right bookshelves and discovered many new translations of Kashmiri texts. And Tom Weaver went still further and traced, by computer, a series of manuscripts whose contents have provided a scriptural confirmation of some very personal experiences.

I am grateful to Timeless Books for the production of this book, and will feel much rewarded if it helps and inspires others.

A Word from the Author

When it came time to reprint *Gods Who Walk the Rainbow,* it seemed a perfect opportunity to expand upon it, and the result is this new edition, *In the Company of the Wise.* I have added three new chapters to Part One, including recent reflections on my personal guru, Swami Sivananda, and the stories of my meetings with Sai Baba of Shirdi, and with the Catholic stigmatist, Padre Pio.

I have also expanded Part Two to include my current thinking on aspirants' illusions, pseudo-gurus, and the responsibilities of gurus and disciples in their relationship. New material and previously published work were woven together. For reference purposes, I have added a glossary, an expanded bibliography, and a directory to the centers of each teacher I write about. When all the proposed changes were assembled it seemed best to rename the book and publish it on its own merit.

My interest has recently been ignited by a new perspective on my relationship with Swami Sivananda. For the first time I have attempted to let something of our past be known, in the hope of helping others understand the possibility of dimensions beyond those we normally accept.

When I first went to India I had only an intellectual concept of space and time, with a few glimpses of a very "other" dimension. I was surprised when Swami Sivananda would introduce me to people as "my friend from Kashmir," or would sometimes call me "auntie." Only when I was leaving India did he state in his farewell address that "we had lived together and worked together in the field of spirituality in a past life."

Now in this book, I explore not only space and time—many good scientific works will do that—but also the possibility of a personal relationship between the same "consciousnesses" that once inhabited different bodies and lived in different cultures in quite another time. I pursue a thread that seems to lead into the distance, where there are only resting places but there is never an end.

Although I have felt cautious about presenting what the rational mind might find irrational, the facts of my experience will have to speak for themselves. Sometimes we have to trust in the Light so firmly that hesitations and doubts roll off like beads of water from a lotus leaf.

Foreword

As I read this book I was interested to find out *how* Swami Radha learned from these spiritual teachers and saints, not just *what* she learned. She brought to each encounter a lively curiosity, an openness to the guru, and an awareness of her own heart and mind. The curiosity came from a sincere and deep desire to find out what she could learn from the teacher. The openness was a willingness to put aside presuppositions, and to receive as fully as possible the teachings and spiritual wisdom.

The awareness of her own heart and mind allowed her to be honest with questions, doubts, concerns. She acknowledged her fears rather than dismiss them or suppress them. She asked questions, even foolish or "ignorant" ones. She wondered about her ability to believe without reason or logic to support her. It is useful to know that these thoughts are natural even in a spiritually experienced person.

We can learn from her example. One must develop discernment in selecting a spiritual guru, just as with any other teacher or mentor. One must learn to recognize the authentic teachers among the many who have only emotional enthusiasm or who serve their own egos rather than the Higher Self. The respected Swami Sivananda of Rishikesh was Swami Radha's own guru, and she was ordained by him into the order of sanyas. Her guidelines on how to choose a guru come from her work with him and her meetings with the many teachers described in this book.

We are seeing increased interest in personal spiritual development in the West. Many persons seek an integration of body, mind, and spirit, whether through joining traditional religious groups, exploring new spiritual movements, or engaging in individual study. Some people may find that they are called to study with a guru, others may choose a different path. These stories by Swami Radha expand our understanding of gurus—what kinds of persons they are, how we can relate to them, and what we can learn from such teachers. There are many ways to move toward the Divine in ourselves and in others, and as we do so we learn to respond to the Divine in any form.

ARTHUR HASTINGS
Professor
Institute of Transpersonal Psychology
Menlo Park, California

Introduction

During my two trips to the East, I was fortunate to meet a number of exceptional teachers who helped me in my personal development and in laying the groundwork for my own teachings. In the first part of this book, I describe my encounters with these sages. Each guru whom I met demonstrated a different approach by which he or she reached a high level of spiritual attainment. From my own efforts over the past thirty-five years to put these teachings into action, I also want to offer a realistic foundation for others who are sincerely seeking enlightenment. So in Part II I explore the nature of spiritual learning, describe the relationship between guru and disciple, and give some guidelines to distinguish true gurus from false ones.

My first journey to the Orient in 1955 was primarily to Rishikesh, India, in the foothills of the Himalayas, where I received initiation into *sanyas*[1] from Swami Sivananda. In my book *Radha: Diary of a Woman's Search,* I describe this intensive spiritual journey. In the present work I complete the picture of my first trip to India by writing about others I

[1] Sanyas is the renunciation of action based on desire. It also refers to a formal initiation of a disciple into a life of selfless service.

met at the time, including my music and dance gurus, and the Tibetan guru who was to have such an impact on my future work.

My return to the West was very difficult. I needed to find a place to assess my experiences, clear my thinking, and somehow prepare to live once again in the Western culture with its very different demands. Existing *ashrams*[2] were few and I was refused refuge even as a temporary guest. Christian communities seemed to be afraid of me because I was a *sanyasi.*[3] Not only did I wear a bright orange sari, but I had been trained in a "heathen" tradition. I was amazed at the arrogance of those who presumed to know the will of the immeasurable power that created the cosmos, the galaxies, and our little planet Earth. When we cannot fathom even the distance of a few billion light years between two stars, how can we dare to define precisely what this Divine Power is and what it wants?

Although I wanted no more responsibility than I felt able to handle, my unusual way of living and my orange robe attracted a number of people. They found a place to meet and hold *satsang.*[4] When our meeting place became too small, we moved into an old house that became our first ashram. In this way I began to fulfil my guru's instructions to start ashrams and centers throughout North America. I found that even with the blessings of my guru, it was not easy to carry out his commands. There were a number of difficulties that I had to learn to deal with entirely through my own experience. To run an ashram from a sense of duty was not enough. Love had to become my motivation, and it tended to fluctuate.

In 1958 I returned to Sivananda Ashram and to my guru, Swami Sivananda. I also had the opportunity to meet the many other spiritual teachers I describe here, and to make a pilgrimage to several Buddhist temples and monasteries throughout the Orient. The additional contact helped me clarify the immense amount of learning that had been so compressed in my first trip, and helped me to re-establish balance.

Certain practices that I participated in, such as walking for sixty hours without sleep or a proper meal, were very vigorous and brought me to a point of near collapse, clearly showing me my physical and

---

[2] An ashram is a spiritual center created when disciples, who are attracted to a guru, begin to gather and live around him or her.

[3] A sanyasi is a renunciate whose life is devoted to the service of humanity.

[4] Satsang refers to a time when seekers gather to chant, meditate, or worship together. Literally it means "the company of the wise."

emotional limits. That I survived these and other intense practices was due to the preparation of enduring six and a half years of war, when sleep had to be snatched standing upright in the shelters during air attacks; and to the fact that Swami Sivananda, before my first visit, had demanded that I learn to sit for five hours motionless. That discipline, as well as reciting a four-line mantra a thousand times a day for forty-five days, was certainly training that saved me from physical and emotional collapse during the practices I was given on this second visit to the East.

We cannot really understand the mind until we reach its limits of physical and emotional resistance, and recognize its creative powers. Under stress the mind will conjure up strange visions that we in the West call psychic phenomena, although my various disciplinarian monks did not call them that. When all the wheels have turned, all the emotions spilled over—fear, despair, hopelessness—the mind reaches a point where it cannot create solutions, even impossible or ridiculous ones. That moment, when there is nothing left to think or do, is the moment of surrender. (Winston Churchill experienced this state when England was under air attack and had no protection. In the instant of complete surrender, when he forgot even to suck on his cigar, the idea of the radar system came to him.) The yogi intentionally creates this state of mind and emotions to allow intuitive perceptions to emerge.

I hope this book will inspire others to tap their own mental resources and to keep that spark of learning alive. In Part I, you will meet me as an aspirant, travelling throughout the Orient, interacting with different gurus, questioning, struggling to overcome preconceived ideas, and to further my spiritual development. In Part II, I speak from what I have learned about the guru-disciple relationship and the process of learning. But I cannot say I was once a student and now I am a teacher. Without continuing to learn, I could not teach. As human beings we are to different degrees a student and to different degrees a teacher, at different phases in our lives. In the same way, we cannot say we are only physical beings or we are only spiritual beings. As long as we live, we move between two worlds; so throughout our lives we have to look into our mental basements, as well as into our mental heavens. Eventually, when we have come to accept both, we realize that the Power behind them is one.

Swami Sivananda Radha

Part ONE

Remembering My Teachers

CHAPTER 1

WHAT IS A GURU?

In the general sense a guru is a teacher—teaching anything from music, to language, to the interpretation of scriptural texts. In the intimate sense, a guru is the person who awakens others to their spiritual search, helping them to keep the spiritual flame alive and to fan it to a greater intensity for Self-Realization. The guru, as spiritual teacher, has the goal of serving the Most High, being a channel of the Light, inspiring disciples to levels beyond thought. The physical manifestation of the guru—when the term *guru* is applied in its true meaning—will be only a steppingstone to the discovery of the Divine within, or what Swami Sivananda called "the guru of all gurus."

Spiritual aspirants are persons who have recognized a higher purpose than living "the good life." They seek a spiritual guru to help free themselves from limitations, and to help them realize their human potential and ultimately their own Self.

In the sense that a guru can be anyone or anything from whom one learns, both my father and my husband were gurus to me. My father wisely encouraged me, from a very early age, to be an independent thinker. He patiently listened when I wrote little stories, and had an effective way of teaching a small child. I particularly remember his lesson about jealousy. My father liked dogs and had sometimes two or three at a time. One day he fed and patted one dog and showed me how the other dog was terribly jealous, growling, showing his teeth, and trying to frighten away the one he was patting. Then he fed, stroked, and patted the jealous dog, and the first one reacted in the same way.

Father looked up and said, "Sylvia, never lower yourself to the level of a dog. While animals have instincts and are not stupid, they lack a certain type of reasoning. Even though I was showing both of them my love with words and by feeding and caressing them equally, they did not realize that they had no need for jealousy. Human beings can think and reason, so there is never any excuse to display jealousy."

My husband was also a guru in this sense. From him I learned a special quality of love. One evening he invited some of his friends to our house. They brought flowers for me, in the traditional European way of showing respect to the hostess. However, my husband displayed a rather negative mood for which I felt obliged to make up. I think he had forgotten that he had invited them and somehow their coming did not suit him. I quickly placed the flowers in a very simple container so that I could give my attention to the visitors.

After they were gone, I spied a suitable vase that happened to be on top of the library shelf. I tried to reach it by standing on my toes. My husband, who was lying on the couch, got up and said, "Why didn't you ask me?" I told him that because of his bad mood I would not have dared to ask him for any favors. If he was moody in front of his own guests, I thought I would have to be very careful.

Then he asked me to sit down with him, poured a sherry, and explained that his viewpoint was quite different. He felt that one could always make new friends and acquaintances.

"But with you," he said, "I live my whole life. I can't make you the target of a mood I cannot control. Our guests will forget, and if they don't, it doesn't matter. But you are my wife and we are sharing our lives with each other, therefore I am very careful not to treat you disrespectfully or make you the target of my moods."

This lesson I have passed on to a number of couples who were having marital difficulties. A breakdown in relationships often comes from carelessness, from taking the partner for granted and not expressing love or respect. As the years have passed, I have tried more and more to look upon everything and everyone as a guru in this ordinary sense.

In India, however, I clearly saw that the word *guru* took on a more rigorous meaning when applied to a spiritual teacher. Swami Sivananda of Rishikesh explains it as follows: "The word *guru* contains two letters, *gu* and *ru. Gu* means 'darkness' and *ru* means 'the dispeller.' Being the dispeller of the darkness of ignorance, the spiritual teacher is called guru."

According to Dr. Judith Tyberg's book of mystical and philosophic Sanskrit terms, *The Language of the Gods, guru* means, "A spiritual preceptor or guide (*Guru*—heavy, venerable, from the verb-root *gri*—to invoke, to praise). A Guru in India is one who has the capacity to pass on his realizations to those who seek him for wisdom. There may be the outer Guru or Guide who removes ignorance by the radiant light of his divine wisdom, or the inner Guru or Atman (Self) who is the spiritual Guide working through the intuitive part of man."[1]

Swami Sivananda was my guru—the master who initiated me, the mother who gave birth to my spiritual life. To him I owe the greatest debt of gratitude. In the following pages I have included one specific story about him, but I really needed a whole book[2] to describe his influence on my life.

Because I had this very intimate relationship with Swami Sivananda, I feel all the gurus I have met were part of my spiritual destiny. My interactions with them did not turn me away from Gurudev Sivananda, but instead helped to reinforce my relationship with him. By seeing that all these teachers had different approaches, different ways of teaching, different "powers" if you like, I realized that in Sivananda I had found the right teacher.

Many of my meetings with other gurus were arranged by Swami Sivananda himself, to expose me to their particular influences. When you are a disciple and your guru sends you to meet other gurus, it is a very different experience from pursuing others because you are dissatisfied with what you have. For example, when Purushottamananda came to Sivananda Ashram, Gurudev called and arranged for me to visit his cave. When a disciple of Papa Ramdas visited, Sivananda said of Ramdas, "We have not met in person, but we meet often in the heart," and for

---

[1] Tyberg, *The Language of the Gods,* 3.

[2] Radha, *Radha: Diary of a Woman's Search.*

that reason he wanted me to meet him. Again, the opportunity to be with Anandamayi Ma was set up by Swami Sivananda.

Some of the meetings with other gurus seemed to arrange themselves, or as I see it, "my Divine Committee" arranged them for me. For example, I never intended to meet Meher Baba—in fact, I didn't even know of his existence until a woman I had just met insisted I should see him, and presented the opportunity that I describe later.

By my attitude, by my way of questioning, and by responding to the questions of these spiritual teachers, I experienced something essential of them. But unless we are loyal to our first commitment, we will not necessarily have such experiences.

To all of these gurus I owe the gratitude that I have deeply felt. I have kept my accounts to a minimum to let the reader contact each one of them in the way it is meant to be. It is not possible to describe precisely what one experiences in the presence of a saintly person, but I hope that what is conveyed will be a help, even an inspiration, to others who embark on their spiritual journey.

RESOURCES FOR THE READER

Suggested Reading

RADHA, SWAMI SIVANANDA. *Radha: Diary of a Woman's Search.* 2d ed Palo Alto: Timeless Books, 1990.

SIVANANDA, SWAMI. *Guru and Disciple.* Sivananda Nagar, Rishikesh: Divine Light Society, 1955.

TYBERG, JUDITH. *The Language of the Gods.* Los Angeles: East-West Cultural Center, 1970.

Audio Tape

RADHA, SWAMI SIVANANDA. *Guru and Disciple.* Palo Alto: Timeless Books.

Chapter 2

Ayyapan, the Sadhu, and the Head of Kailas Ashram

One of the people who was most helpful to me at the time of my first visit to Sivananda Ashram was Ayyapan, a tall thin man with long white hair. His living quarters were next to mine and he was staying at the ashram while waiting to receive his initiation into sanyas from Swami Sivananda. A well-educated man who spoke good English, he spent time with me explaining the local customs and taking me to points of interest.

On one occasion when we went to the bazaar in Rishikesh we saw some *sadhus*[1] who were objects of curiosity to the Western tourists. One sadhu seemed to be particularly attractive to the visitors. When they tried to approach him, he bent down, picked up a stone, and threatened to throw it if they did not leave him alone. I found that rather strange behavior. Where was all the gentleness, compassion,

[1] A sadhu is a wandering mendicant; a holy man living a spiritual life independent of any institution.

understanding, and cosmic love I had heard about? It did not seem to be expressed by his attitude.

Later I came to understand that the sadhu does not appreciate being a tourist attraction or being viewed like some strange animal, so he reacts to the denial of his dignity in the only way he thinks he will be understood.

One day on our way to Gurudev's garden, which was a few miles outside Rishikesh, Ayyapan and I were sitting in one of the coffee stalls that opened onto the road. The same sadhu I had seen earlier in Rishikesh came and sat next to me, looking at me in a very friendly way. Then he started to talk, asking me what I was doing in India. Before I could find words, Ayyapan explained that I had come from Canada to learn about the teachings and that I was a disciple of Swami Sivananda. He gave him all sorts of information that I thought superfluous, because I remembered the attitude of this sadhu very well. However, his friendliness finally encouraged me to ask him why he had threatened to throw a stone at the people the other day.

He said, "Oh, they are curiosity seekers. They only want to take pictures. They don't understand anything. People come from places like *Life* magazine to photograph us. They distort what they hear, and because of their lack of sensitivity and knowledge, they severely criticize our saintly teachers."

"Don't they pay for permission to take your picture? Some journalists are expected to pay as much as fifty rupees for that."

He shook his head and said, "No, I do not let them take my picture. I would not sell my reputation for fifty rupees to one of these dumb-heads."

I asked him what he thought about the Indian dancers who go to America to perform and give a taste of Indian culture. He felt that this was wrong and said, "The Westerners only want to be entertained. They are not really interested. They don't want to work; they don't have the stamina."

I interjected, "Do you think that they are all softies?"

He laughed heartily. He thought that was a marvelous word, and said, "Softies! Yes, that's better than calling them dumb-heads. They are softies, they are sensation- seekers. Anyhow, those Indians who go to America are often the ones who don't really know what they're doing, or else they make adjustments for the limited understanding of the Western audience."

Certainly the Indian artists who had come to Sivananda Ashram seemed to be of a different caliber from those I had seen in Europe or America.

I asked the sadhu if he would tell me something about the *nagas* because one of them was sitting near us. He explained, "They are a sect of sadhus who wear no clothing once they have attained a certain stage of spiritual development. It takes a long time before a man can achieve enough control over his sexual instincts to remain cool and unstimulated even when he sees the most beautiful woman. Only those who have achieved that control are permitted to be naked. They show in this way that there is nothing to hide."

The naga who was sitting there, drinking something I couldn't recognize, looked at me and smiled with great warmth in his eyes. He seemed to be listening to our conversation, and sometimes I could see surprise reflected on his face. I did not know if this was because of my limited understanding, or the way I posed my questions, or whether he felt that the answers that the sadhu gave me were insufficient. But he was definitely participating through his listening, even though he remained silent.

Then the sadhu told me a story about Sri Ramakrishna who was deluged with people from all over India, wanting to be his disciples, seeking his initiation.

"Ramakrishna took them to the Ganges," he said, "and had them step into the water with him, waist high. Then, with an unexpected movement, since he was a small and very slightly-built man, he grabbed their hair with a firm grip, pushed them under the water and let them struggle for breath, allowing them to come up for air just at the last minute. Then he said, 'When you want God as badly as you have just now struggled for your life, you can come back.'"

The sadhu smiled, "I just pick up a stone to send people away. Someone who is not frightened away, I will of course have to look over."

I asked, "Why am I so fortunate that you will even talk to me?"

He said, "I have seen you in various places and people say that you are very obedient to your guru, Swami Sivananda, and never quarrel with him. This tells me that you want to learn, that you want to know."

Then he told me where his cave was located and said Ayyapan could take me there if I had any questions that Gurudev Sivananda did not have enough time to answer. Ayyapan seemed to understand the description, because he nodded his head saying, *"Atcha, atcha,"* which means a hundred thousand things for the Indians. It means "Yes, yes"; it means "How interesting!"; it means "That's almost unbelievable!"; it can mean "How come?"; it can mean "Surprising, surprising!"

I now asked the sadhu, "How can anyone see God in a snake? The last time I went to the bathing *ghat*,[2] I saw a huge python. Some people didn't seem bothered by the snake, but I had to exercise tremendous self-control just to overcome my fear. Now that I can allow fish in the Ganges to eat out of my hands, do you think that someday I could transfer that same trust to a python?"

Just when I realized that my questions were accumulating like beads on a string, he said, "It's getting dark—you have to go back now. But when you have 108 questions together, like 108 beads on a *mala*,[3] come and bring them all or, even better, write them down." He smiled and said, "I might answer them all, or just some—we'll see!" And with "Om Namah Sivaya," he departed.

I could see that my list of questions for the sadhu could be quite long if I ever had a chance to accept his offer and visit his cave. Unfortunately, he lived on the other side of the Ganges, which meant walking all the way to Lakshmanjula and over the suspension bridge. (The big sign at the entrance to the bridge, "Elephants, camels, and automobiles not permitted," always amused me.) I was sorry that I did not have the opportunity to take advantage of his invitation.

As we were walking back to Sivananda Ashram, I could not help expressing my surprise to Ayyapan that the sadhu had been so friendly, and that he had given us the location of his hideaway. Ayyapan did not find the sadhu's friendliness surprising, but felt that my questions had convinced him of my serious interest. The sadhu was in contact with various disciples at Sivananda Ashram, and, Ayyapan said, "He may have heard that you are very eager, and that you have adapted beautifully to our way of living and the simplicity of the ashram. Perhaps it is also that you have been here for some time, while most people just pass through after a few days."

That puzzled me. Why would anyone come to India without having some serious purpose? Why particularly would they come to Rishikesh, or any of the places where people gather to pursue God or Self-Realization in so many different and sometimes strange ways? I would not waste the time and money unless I thought I could get what I wanted.

---

[2] A ghat is a series of steps going down to the water.

[3] A mala is a string of 108 beads, used in reciting one of the names of the Divine.

Swami Radha's companion and guide, Ayyapan (on the right with the white beard) with the manager of Kailas Ashram. "The manager was intrigued by my presence, because very few Westerners had ever visited this ashram."

Ayyapan also explained that because of the ideal of non-killing, which is shared by all holy people in India, "We find some Westerners insensitive when they wear leather or fur without any thought about it." Suddenly he looked at me and asked, "But you don't wear any leather?"

"No. I made my shoulder-bag out of cloth and bought shoes of a synthetic fabric; the material that I brought for Gurudev's coat is really a very light nylon pile, which looks like fur and has the warmth of fur. Before I came to India I had contacted some Indian friends in Canada and found out about the customs of your country."

Ayyapan seemed very pleased that I understood, and that I wanted to express my respect for this different culture.

And it was a *very* different culture. It amazed me how in a place as small as Rishikesh there could be people following so many different religions, ways of worship, and studies of scripture. I found out more about this on another adventure with Ayyapan.

I frequently went with Ayyapan to Rishikesh to buy fruit or imported canned food at the bazaar because I was unable to eat the spicy Indian food. Around the bazaar were many other buildings besides the little hovels in which the merchants lived, and I often wondered who occupied these.

On one of our shopping trips Ayyapan took me into one of the buildings, which I found was Kailas Ashram, a *kshetra*[4] set up to look after sadhus from the Rishikesh area and to help destitute pilgrims who encounter many hardships and difficulties on their pilgrimages.

The manager was intrigued by my presence, because very few Westerners had ever visited this ashram. He showed us around a beautiful library where I saw books such as I had never seen before: bundles of loose sheets of paper pressed between two wooden plates, elaborately illustrated. They were lying on shelves that reached from floor to ceiling, ancient texts, many of which I am sure had never been translated.

We were taken around the kshetra, and as we passed the doors of different rooms the manager explained that the kshetra catered to sadhus of various backgrounds and different customs. Often the way they decorated their bodies indicated which aspect of the Divine they worshipped. Some seemed to be highly educated while others were very simple. In some of the rooms sadhus ate completely undressed, according to their tradition, while others had to be fully clothed. Some

[4] A kshetra is a resting place for pilgrims to stop on their way to Mt. Kailas, the holy mountain in the Himalayas.

Pilgrims, sadhus, and those in need receive the generous offerings of food and medication from the *kshetra*.

could eat only a certain type of food, others only at a certain hour of the day, and so on, according to the regulations of the school of thought or religious sect from which they came. I could not see how such customs had anything to do with building character, but that was a very superficial assessment. In order to really understand I would have to immerse myself in the tradition and discipline, and then perhaps a different picture would emerge.

The manager insisted that he introduce me to the head of Kailas Ashram, a man of indeterminable age. He was sitting on one large cushion, with others piled around him. Ayyapan explained that this was a kind of throne, symbolizing his position as head of the ashram. As we were sitting silently in front of this holy man, I saw that most of the time he sat with his eyes half closed and his lips moving constantly, although I could hear no sound. Occasionally he would question me, but because he spoke in Hindi, Ayyapan had to translate.

On the wall above him was an image of Divine Mother. Again Ayyapan explained, telling me that Divine Mother has 108 names and is worshipped as the Mother of Creation. But he cautioned that it would take time for me to understand how the different aspects of Divine Mother correspond to the many stages of the development of the universe and to the evolution of consciousness.

Several times I returned to Kailas Ashram, but only on invitation since I did not want to overstep any rules. I learned that the the kshetra supported both the physical and educational needs of those searching for a higher purpose in their lives. Food, medicine, and maps for pilgrimages were provided for wandering sadhus, students, and pilgrims, to assist their efforts in seeking the Light. There were eighty-five huts that served as shelters and as places of spiritual retreat for their wide range of intensive practices and disciplines. A Sanskrit college had been opened for those who wished to increase their knowledge of scriptures and ancient written teachings, and books were freely distributed. Rooms for contemplation and study were provided.

Through unsolicited donations, the kshetra also generously supported Indians in need. Food and medical services went to the deserving poor, to lepers, to victims of floods and famines, and to refugees exiled from their homeland—in short, wherever relief could be given. Although it was not in the regulations, the generosity of this place extended even to widows, whose lot in India is not an easy one. This kindness was most unusual because the Indian woman who has outlived her husband is often viewed with suspicion, and is thought to be unworthy of protection. The selfless service carried out by the ashram was an inspiration to all who were seeking the light of understanding and compassion.

When the time came for me to leave India, I went to say good-by to the head of the ashram, who had been so kind to me. He motioned me to sit down, then called one of his disciples to bring all the rose petals from the morning worship of Divine Mother. Neither Ayyapan nor I had told him the purpose of our visit, but the old man seemed to know. With a most beautiful smile, he handed all the petals to me, saying, "These are the rose petals from the worship of Divine Mother. You are her most beloved child. Serve her well in your country. Open your doors for her children. Radiate love. Inspire all her children to come back to their heavenly home. People are like truants who have run away."

Then picking up his mala, he wrapped it around his arm several times like a bracelet. By now I knew why he moved his lips: he was reciting a *mantra*,[5] probably one of the 108 names of Divine Mother. He said, "Every day for a year I will recite a mala for blessings and divine support for you, because the work that you do in the West will be very hard, with many difficulties. People's hearts have become stone, their ears have become closed, and they have lost sight of the purpose of life."

His voice and his face expressed such concern that I could not help feeling fearful as I wondered what these difficulties would be. I still believed that everything I received had to be earned, and it was a new experience for me to find that he would give me this great spiritual gift and expect nothing in return. I felt gratitude welling up in me for his acceptance, love, and concern.

He took from his neck a beautiful garland of fresh flowers that he had worn for the morning's celebration, put this over my head, and placed his palms together in the reverent Indian greeting of "Namaste." Although I had had difficulty in accepting myself, it was impossible not to accept this salutation to the divinity that was also within me, a moving experience of what had been only theoretical until then. As a Hindu of high position, head of this large ashram, he was greeting me as a bishop of the Western tradition would salute a pilgrim coming to a holy place. All I could do was bow down and touch his feet in the Indian custom, thanking him with the look in my eyes more than with words. Somehow I felt that he understood. I left, carrying with me his warmth and concern, together with the rose petals that I had carefully wrapped in the corner of my silken sari.

On the way back Ayyapan assured me that although I had stumbled with my words of thanks, he understood how moved I was. It is not in the German tradition to talk about what is most precious and sacred, and I began to see how much I had to learn about allowing my feelings to surface and be expressed in words.

Ayyapan spoke about the depth of spiritual friendship that had come through my interaction with the people I had met here in the foothills of the Himalayas. My acceptance of them and eagerness to learn from them meant that they had been able to accept me, and could express their concern—like the head of Kailas Ashram had—in such a beautiful way.

---

[5] A mantra is a combination of sacred syllables that form a nucleus of spiritual energy, and is chanted to achieve single-pointedness of mind.

CHAPTER 3

INDIAN MUSIC TEACHERS

"Music is an essential component of the cultural expression of a country and even a civilization. It is in this sacred land of Aryavarta that music became the vehicle of highest spiritual attainments and Self-Realization, and that is why our ancients interlaced music with worship in temples. The fundamental conception of music is that it is the source of all creation."[1]

This quotation is from Professor Shastri, one of the three men who taught me about the philosophical and practical aspects of Indian music. Professor Shastri, who lectured on modern music on Radio India in New Delhi, was most knowledgeable in the field of classical Indian music. Because he himself was well trained and enthusiastic about his subject, he liked a pupil like I was, eager to know and understand.

He explained that Indian music was never intended to be entertainment, but in the course of time it had descended from its lofty

[1] Unpublished notes from Swami Radha's diary.

Professor Shastri, one of Swami Radha's music teachers. "He made me aware that the vibrations of music could have an effect on the different centers of the body."

spiritual heights to its present-day level. Music for entertainment should not be abolished, he felt, but it should at least lift people from their daily drudgery to joy. However the potential and ultimate aim of practicing Indian music is to aspire to the omnipresent sound of "Aum," which transforms even an uneducated person into a state of Higher Consciousness.

According to Indian tradition, mantra was not invented by human beings but was intuitively perceived by the *rishis*[2] and later translated by them into sound as we know it. Mantras have been used by countless generations of seekers as a way to Self-Realization.

Man-made music, or struck music, is called *sangita* and is in contrast to the unstruck sound, the cosmic Aum, which cannot be heard at

---

[2] A rishi is a seer, visionary, or spiritual individual of great sensitivity.

Swami Nadabrahmananda. "All the mantras and bhajans that I sing personally and that are now used at Yasodhara Ashram have their origin with Nadabrahmananda."

will. The practices using mantra to develop concentration and to become single-pointed, form the steps that eventually lead to the peak experience of hearing the cosmic Aum.

Professor Shastri talked to me about the power of mantras and gave me information about the practice, showing me how to use the human voice like a violin, from the very soft to the most powerful. He made me aware that the vibrations of music could have an effect on the different centers of the body. Swami Nadabrahmananda, my music guru at the ashram, demonstrated how these vibrations can be moved to various parts of the body. Because Swami Nadabrahmananda spoke no English, Professor Shastri's explanations were especially helpful.

> All art and education are concentrated in *brahmavidya* (the science of the Absolute or Infinite). Mathematics, metaphysics, and music are the three great disciplines that lead in an ascending order of merit to the Infinite. Indian music has the backbone of mathematics and the soul of metaphysics, preserving its unique melody to appeal to the heart as well as to the head.[3]

---

[3] Unpublished notes from Swami Radha's diary.

Professor Shastri described Indian music as having "the backbone of mathematics and the soul of metaphysics, preserving its unique melody to appeal to the heart as well as the head."

Indian music is said to reflect the structure not only of this world, but of the entire universe. Between two Western tones there is a hierarchy of semitones and demitones, so that an octave of Western music is divided into sixty-six to seventy-two tones. The combinations of these tones are called *ragas* or *raginis*[4] and their delicate mixture produces harmony, not only with each other, but with the melody of nature. The raga-ragini system of sound-vibration was arranged according to the seasons, or to the vibrations peculiar to each season.

The interrelationship and sequences of sound are governed by very strict rules, and each of the ragas, at the moment it is sounded by the human voice or an instrument, is claimed to be in perfect harmony

---

[4] Raga (male) and ragini (female) symbolize melodies in Indian music that are governed by precise rules.

Swami Radha's music guru, Swami Nadabrahmananda, teaching her to play Indian instruments.

with the vibration of the universe. Some ragas are to be performed only in the evening or at specified hours of the day, and others only at certain times of the year. The power that is attributed to the ragas has led to many stories, some of which Professor Shastri told me to help me remember his explanations.

As Professor Shastri said, "There is a good deal of resemblance between the moods of nature and the moods of man. Certain ragas correspond to the zodiacal signs; others can cure ailments like rheumatism, and even heartache."

His explanation of this complex interrelationship opened up to me a whole new way of thinking about sound. Later, when I was practicing one mantra over an extended period of time to achieve single-pointedness, his explanations nourished me as I struggled with the impasses of my mind, and helped me to receive the full benefit of the mantra.

Gopalacharya, who demonstrated that the power of emotions can be transformed through chanting mantras. "Several times during the lessons my attention was caught by a radiance like a huge white disk around his body."

Swami Nadabrahmananda spent hours teaching me mantras and *bhajans,*[5] and instructing me in the playing of the ektar, the tampura, the sitar, and Indian drums. Not only did he show great patience in helping me to train my voice, but he was genuinely happy about every little success I achieved. All the mantras and bhajans that I sing personally and that are now used at Yasodhara Ashram have their origin with Nadabrahmananda.[6]

Gopalacharya was another teacher who contributed to my deeper understanding of the power of mantras. While I was staying with an Indian family in Bombay, they invited me to meet their guru, and suggested that I might like to receive lessons from him in Sanskrit and spiritual texts. Gopalacharya was a kind person, humble and simple, although highly educated in scriptures.

---

[5] Bhajans are songs celebrating an aspect of the Divine.

[6] For more on Swami Nadabrahmananda, see *Radha: Diary of a Woman's Search.*

Swami Radha practicing Indian dance and rhythms with accompaniment from Swami Nadabrahmananda and Swami Venkatesananda.

Several times during the lessons my attention was caught by a radiance like a huge white disk around his body. At first I thought it was a reflection from some source of light, but when he moved, this disk also moved. I made great efforts to listen carefully, because I had a genuine interest in what he was presenting, but I was distracted by this light. Fortunately one of the daughters of my host was busily taking notes, and I pinned my hopes on being able to copy them.

Gopalacharya demonstrated chanting to us by using various intonations of *Gopala,* the name of the child Krishna, and told us something about this aspect of the Divine. Because the child Krishna was as naughty as other little boys, the story goes that he teased the *gopis,*[7] and

[7] Gopis are maidens who tend the cows.

stole the milk and cream from their pitchers. In imitation of this mischievous and demanding child calling his mother, Gopalacharya intoned, "Gopala," his voice sometimes crying, sometimes angry and hurt. He expressed frustration, willfulness, great joy, happiness, laughter, and tears. There was no specific melody. He sometimes started in a deep tone and went very high, just repeating the name Gopala, sometimes with the full strength of his lungs, at other times very softly. Finally his voice sounded like a child's falling asleep, and then he fell silent.

My emotional reactions to his demonstration were not as plentiful as those he expressed, but certainly were wide-ranging. How could anyone repeat a holy name that represents God, in a voice giving vent to the whole spectrum of human emotions? Was this not an insult? I swayed between feeling guilty for having accepted his invitation to join in, and being carried away with watching the disk of light around him. That the tempo was sometimes slow and sometimes fast, was acceptable to me, but anger and resentment and what appeared to me willful demand . . . surely one could not dream of getting away with that!

Someone else in the group felt the same way, and brought up the question that I did not have the courage to voice. Gopalacharya explained that if God has indeed created everything, then that power also has created the emotions and the voice with which to express them, and so it is right to use the voice to give them back. It is much better to get involved with the Divine in this way, he said, than to ignore the Divine entirely. I was not so sure that I could accept that; I would have to think about it.

I was trying to record his teaching on a tape recorder, but there was a strange static that made the machine ineffective. It was much later that I realized he might have been electrically charged by what is commonly called an aura, a large field of energy around him. Perhaps his chanting had created that very clear energy field. After class I waited until the others had gone, then turned to him to apologize and explain what had happened to my concentration.

He understood and told me that everybody has such an auric field, but that it becomes visible only when a certain strength of heart and mind is attained, and when speech expresses a harmony with heart and mind. "If you practice the exercise of the Light, you will create such an aura around yourself. This exercise will purify your mind and heart." This was all said in a quiet tone, in a very matter-of-fact manner.

Gopalacharya also told me that the human ear must hear the human voice, so the mantra must be chanted aloud to reveal the fluctuations, finally reaching the point where the voice becomes clear and sweet, freed from emotional overtones. This is the best way to remove the mental background noises, and is one of the main techniques that yogis practice and teach. He said that by chanting the holy name, seekers can express their emotions without turning them back on themselves and creating more pain and agony; eventually they may experience the Divine Power in the mantra.

This one visit with Gopalacharya brought much of value to my future work, and his instructions have been passed on to great numbers of seekers in North America.

RESOURCES FOR THE READER

Suggested Reading

RADHA, SWAMI SIVANANDA. *Mantras: Words of Power.* Palo Alto: Timeless Books, 1980.

SIVANANDA, SWAMI. *Music as Yoga.* Rishikesh: Divine Life Society, 1956.

Song Books

Bhajans at Yasodhara Ashram. Palo Alto: Timeless Books, 1989.

Mantras, Bhajans, and Songs. Kootenay Bay: Yasodhara Ashram Society, 1979.

Audio Tapes

NADABRAHMANANDA, SWAMI. *Bhajan Party.* Palo Alto: Timeless Books.

NADABRAHMANANDA, SWAMI. *The Science of Thaan.* Palo Alto: Timeless Books.

SIVANANDA, SWAMI, and SWAMI NADABRAHMANANDA. *Sounds of Sivananda Ashram,* recorded by Swami Radha in 1956. Palo Alto: Timeless Books.

SWAMI SIVANANDA RADHA. *Mantras: Songs of Yoga.* Palo Alto: Timeless Books.

SWAMI SIVANANDA RADHA. *Power of Mantras.* Palo Alto: Timeless Books.

Centers

INDIA

Divine Life Society, Sivanandanagar, 249 192 U.P.

CANADA

Yasodhara Ashram, Box 9, Kootenay Bay, B.C. V0B 1X0

Chapter 4

Indian Dance Teacher~ Mr. Devasatyam

Just as I had learned that classical Indian music is sacred, I was also to learn that classical Indian dance is devotional, a physical offering to the Divine. Although I had been a professional dancer in Germany and Canada, and had learned the ritual dances of many countries including India, I realized that the spirit of the dance had not been communicated to me as it was by Mr. Devasatyam.

When I was staying at Sivananda Ashram the first time, my guru arranged for me to take dance lessons from Mr. Devasatyam. He was a guest teacher at a little college in Dehra Dun that was promoting various forms of Indian art in order to keep them alive and to develop them. Mr. Devasatyam was the type of instructor who had very good technical and theoretical knowledge, but who no longer believed in the old traditions. In a dull and dry manner, he would describe to me what I should do, never demonstrating, only correcting. It was a cumbersome way of learning, and although I tried to tape all his instructions, it did not prove to be very helpful.

Mr. Devasatyam and his family accepted Swami Sivananda's invitation to visit the ashram. "Although his visit had been prompted by curiosity, there was now respect and greater understanding of his own traditions."

When in spite of his attitude I learned the dances he was supposed to teach me, he could only shake his head in wonder because his own people could not master the intricacy of the movements in such a short period. Ten years was considered the time necessary to learn the dances perfectly. I told him that I had learned them in a month by the grace of my guru, an idea he found impossible to accept.

He taught what is loosely termed "Indian dancing," but all of the Bharata Natyam dances are individual prayers in which the devotee uses various movements to express thanks to the Divine for having a healthy body for spiritual development. Perhaps it is similar to King David in the Old Testament, singing and dancing before the Lord. Dance can be

Mr. Devasatyam teaching Indian dance to Swami Radha. "Indian dance is one of the best ways to build a bridge to the Divine while human emotions still need to be expressed."

a natural expression of pure joy, of well-being, and gratitude for the beauty and blessings of life.

The symbolic movements of Indian dance are emphasized through words that are spoken aloud or felt inwardly, such as, "The purpose of these arms and hands—although they can work and caress, and although they can punish and be violent—is to be of service to thee." The words and melody are traditional. In this process, speech is refined and the senses are cultivated. In many dances the Divine is personified, and by learning to embody the different divine aspects as presented by the ancient myths, the dancer can begin to understand the particular power of each aspect.

Some of the Indian dances are really a refined form of yoga, where subtle movements with the fingers, the hands, the head, and the body speak a symbolic language. Yoga is dance, and dance is indeed a means of praying. It is one of the best ways to build a bridge to the Divine while human emotions still need to be expressed. For the *brahmachari*[1] dance is a most positive physical outlet, a way to use the body as a spiritual tool for devotion and reverence.

It is possible that this art form was developed at some point in the awakening of human consciousness, as one way to invoke the personal interest of the greater Powers, by pleading with them and offering this gift of devotion instead of an animal or human sacrifice.

The effects of sound and movement are used also in the secular world. An army marches to music, and soldiers are encouraged to sing to keep them going when their bodies tire. Such marching songs may offer little inspiration, but the rhythm and words focus energy to carry individuals beyond their normal limits.

It was only later when I tried to teach one of the prayer dances to others that I understood how the movements were actually put into the consciousness of the cells of the body, and how from there they reflected into the consciousness of the mind. I saw the struggle of the students as I had them learn the movements while saying a line of the prayer over and over again: "Humbly I give you my heart in devotion." The few who responded looked as if a light suddenly turned on inside their bodies and was shining through.

When my dance teacher accepted Swami Sivananda's invitation to visit the ashram, Gurudev explained the importance of the Indian

---

[1] A brahmachari is a yogic initiate preparing for a life dedicated to spiritual goals by practicing celibacy and renunciation.

heritage that Mr. Devasatyam was teaching, and the depths of the art. Swamiji also said that no one could have taught these dances to a Western woman in such a short time unless there had been some memory from past lives to be brought to the surface of the consciousness. Mr. Devasatyam was impressed with this explanation, and on leaving he expressed a deep reverence for Gurudev that he did not have when he came. Although the visit had been prompted by curiosity, there was now respect and greater understanding of his own traditions.

So despite the fact that Mr. Devasatyam had earned his living as an instructor of Indian dance at the college, was paid by the government, and had no real interest in its tradition, through him something of the meaning had come across to me. From this I understood that we can receive whatever we open ourselves to. If only the best is desired, less cannot be given. Certainly there are people who indulge in sensational psychic feats, but the important thing is to be open to the Most High, only to the best. Then all the lower psychic manifestations will be avoided.

To use our limbs in dedication to the Most High in prayer and devotion, in gratitude for good health and for having a body in which to live and find a state of Higher Consciousness, is surely the best expression for the body. In this way it can be used for its true purpose, as the bridge to the Divine, and not just for self-expression that will serve the ego and result in rebirth.

RESOURCES FOR THE READER

Suggested Reading—Indian Dance

AMBROSE, KAY. *Classical Dances and Costumes of India.* New Delhi: Oriental Books Reprint Corp., 1980.

WOSIEN, MARIA-GABRIELE. *Sacred Dance: Encounter With the Gods.* London: Thames & Hudson, 1974.

ZARINA, XENIA. *Classic Dances of the Orient.* New York: Crown Publishers, Inc., 1967.

CHAPTER 5

THE TIBETAN GURU

During my first stay at Sivananda Ashram I spent some time with a German family in Dehra Dun where I took lessons in Indian dance. While I was there I went with my hostess to Mussoorie for a few days to have dental work done by one of the few German dentists in the area. As I was out walking one day, absorbed in my thoughts, at a certain point along the road an indescribable view of the Himalayas spread before me. A sense of awe and wonder filled my whole being, all else seemed to vanish, all sense of time was lost.

Finally I continued my walk, still lost in wonder, when I noticed a man coming down the path toward me. When he was a short distance away he looked at me, his eyes capturing mine. His expression was different from the naive, childlike curiosity of so many Indians. He was a slight person, yet commanding; his eyes were deep and there appeared to be a light coming from them. I noted in my diary, "The light was extending from his eyes almost the length of my middle finger." When he came close, they held an expression of love that was indescribable. This love, which seemed superhuman, I had seen in only one other person: Swami Sivananda.

He stopped, smiled, and then nodded his head. As he slowly resumed his walk, I continued on my way in a daze. He had not asked me where I came from or my name, as Indians usually do. I looked down the road after him, but he did not turn. I saw him blending into the sunlight that was coming through the trees, very beautifully, very vividly.

The next time I saw him was when a group of people at the ashram were going to hear a man they described as a wonderful teacher, as well as a saint. They urged me to come along, so I went with four or five others to the hut in Rishikesh where he gave discourses. When we entered the gate to the garden, a class was already in progress and several people were sitting listening to him. He did not pay any attention to us, but finished what he was saying. When he finally did look up and his eyes met mine, my heart leapt with joy—joy at the memory of our first meeting on the path of sunlight and trees in the mountains of Mussoorie.

Those who had been here before quietly sat down. I stood, uncertain, and then asked, "May I sit down?"

He replied, "I have no need of disciples." After the intensity of our initial contact, I was shattered.

Then he continued after a pause, "I am only interested in people of superior intelligence." He turned away from me and went on with his conversation.

I was very much affected and moved slowly toward the garden gate, ready to leave. My mind raced, searching, trying to assess my intelligence. I had never considered myself of superior intelligence. But I somehow intuitively decided to ask him what he meant, so again I turned to face him, and as I was about to speak he said, "A person of superior intelligence is one who can learn from the mistakes of others without making the mistakes herself."

I stood there for a moment thinking. A few incidents came to mind where I had avoided doing something after seeing others make a mistake. I decided to sit down and join the group.

He spoke of the way things become more and more subtle as perception increases on the various levels. He talked of thoughts, the kind of stuff they are made of.

During a moment of silence I blurted out, "Yes, I have always wondered what kind of power that is and why I can't measure it. I know

View from the Mussoorie monastery in the Himalayas, the scene where Swami Radha first saw her Tibetan guru. "A sense of awe and wonder filled my whole being, all else seemed to vanish, all sense of time was lost."

nothing about the power I use to transmit my thoughts into words, and I know little about the power of words."

I had spoken impulsively, having not yet learned the etiquette of asking permission before speaking to a guru. He smiled, obviously overlooking my apparent rudeness, because now he began to discuss the questions that I had brought up.

When his class was over, I was leaving with the others, but he called me and said, "You stay."

He set a time for me to come again the next day, but when I arrived there was no one else there and I thought I had made a mistake. I was ready to leave when he came from behind the house. I did not ask him where the others were. I was so intent on learning and on tuning in that it just did not matter. It did not enter my mind.

We sat in front of the hut on a stone platform, and he went straight to the point just as if he had left off his teaching only a minute before. He continued to speak about the subtleties of perception, of sense impressions, and the idea of *prana.*[1] Sometimes it was not easy for me to understand him, although I found his accent no more difficult than that of many Indians. I have no idea how long I spent with him. I just remember sitting there in utter wonderment, trying to absorb his every word. Suddenly he was at the gate, telling me when we would meet again.

There was never anyone else present whenever I came to see him. I began to understand that I was not to talk about these visits and what I learned, or something would be lost, the Energy dissipated.

Strangely enough, Swami Sivananda had made a similar remark to a visitor in the office, "For the next two years you will not talk about yoga and you will not even let on that you know what the word means. You must starve your ego and your vanity in wanting to show that you, too, know something about yoga."

Then Gurudev continued, seeing the visitor's puzzled look, "In this way you will preserve the Energy, which will become the source from which you can draw." This was the same lesson that I was learning from the Tibetan.

On one of my meetings with him he took from a small cotton bag an uncooked grain of rice and put it into my hand saying, "Now look at it."

I glanced at it. "Yes, this is a grain of rice."

He motioned with his finger at the rice again, indicating that I should look at it longer. Again I looked, thinking he would give me a sign when I should stop. Then, with a slight touch on my wrist, he took the grain of rice and held it between his two slender fingers up against the sky.

He said, "Look at the grain of rice—not my fingers, not the sky." Then he lowered his hand. I don't know what happened to the grain of rice. It probably fell to the ground. Through some strange perception, perhaps through his power, I could see the tiny image of the rice in the sky, and gradually it began to grow. There was a halo of white light around it as it continued to expand. Although my mind had projected it there in the first place, it now seemed to be detached and to take on a life of its own.

---

[1] *Prana* is a very subtle energy travelling with the breath, just as a flower's fragrance travels through the air. Prana can be stored in the body.

Later, when I returned to the ashram, I experienced another of those strange coincidences. Swami Sivananda gave me a book, which I opened to this exercise: "Stand in the sun until your body casts a shadow the same size as you are. Look at the neck of your shadow until your eyes burn, then turn your gaze into the sky and project your image there." I began to wonder about such coincidences and the role the Tibetan yogi was playing in the drama of my life.

I learned from him a number of exercises that were extremely helpful and that I had enough time to practice while I was in India so I would not forget them. Because the body is very teachable, anything that is practiced to the point of mechanicalness is easily recalled.

It was from the Tibetan that I learned the significance of the symbolism of the Kundalini system,[2] the spiritual centers in the spine. He made me aware that there are no actual lotuses like the ones that are shown in books on the subject.

He told me a story of a Chinese merchant who was selling all his goods, but did not want to part with a piece of silken damask. Therefore, he would show only the back, a poor replica of the splendid front that he felt people could not appreciate.

Slowly I came to realize that I would have to learn much more about symbols. As a teacher he could only give me the back view of that beautiful damask of kundalini, because I was not yet ready to understand more. But someday I would grasp it, appreciate it, and maybe then I would get a taste of that state of bliss. Although I do not remember well the details of that story, what is important is that I suddenly had the revelation that I must listen not only with the physical ear and the mind; I must also learn to listen with intuition, with the inner ear. I tried to apply this from then on, and even my relationship with Swami Sivananda improved. My meeting with the Tibetan was indeed a great blessing.

He told me about the importance of imagination and how it leads to desire. Pointing to a picture of a woman with a piece of pottery, he likened the stuff of the mind to the clay. Desire gives it shape and form, and the emotions act like a kiln and cause it to harden. In the continuing process, the clay of the mind loses flexibility and becomes as hard as rock, and then it is almost impossible for it to change. This is like preconceived ideas and other obstacles that are also the creation of the

---

[2] See *Kundalini Yoga for the West.*

mind. Sometimes those concepts have been driven into us as children by the adults who had charge of us, before we had sufficient discrimination. "But now," I realized, "I am an adult, independent, able to think for myself, and responsible for myself."

Every visit to the Tibetan yogi was a surprise and a great learning experience. There were not many conversations between us. He zeroed right in on what he intended to teach me, saying, "I give you three minutes to think about this." He seemed to have a good sense of time, even though I never saw him wearing a watch.

One time he welcomed me with a smile and seemed to be particularly kind and gentle. Then suddenly, quite unexpectedly, he bombarded me with a torrent of questions, giving me no time to think. What he said seemed to be making sense, yet seemed to be utter nonsense. It was like a hammer breaking to bits and pieces all that I believed, all that I needed to hold onto for my emotional and mental security. I felt shattered and exhausted, close to tears, numb and empty.

The second of these "treatments" was worse. When it was all over, after a long silence, he remarked in a gentle, comforting voice, "It was barely an hour. Now the attachments are broken, the door is unlocked. You are free. Move on. Don't look back. Enjoy your freedom."

But I could think only in terms of survival. There were moments when I felt like someone in a small boat in the middle of the ocean. Yes, there was all that space, no limitation, but the waves of a turbulent life still had to be mastered. This new freedom had some very frightening aspects. The mind has an awesome power. How easy it is, if we are only intellectualizing, to say, "Oh, it is all in the mind." How far we are from knowing what we are saying!

Although he never used the word *God,* he never discouraged me from using it. But he told me that temples and churches are only buildings, and the meeting with the Most High, with the Self, was within my own being, in my own spine. On each level of consciousness I could find what I was searching for. I soon became aware that the procedure for understanding and doing this is a matter of training and education. Praying—whether to God or to the guru, the Buddha, or the yogis who have prepared the way—is helpful in order to learn humility, and to realize the limitations of our strength, faith, and ability. This kind of worship made sense to me because it is not worship of any human personality. If I take lessons from a great concert pianist who finally opens the last door into the world of music beyond technique, into the world of sound itself, I will be filled with a great sense of gratitude. Is that not one of the finest emotions to cultivate? We seldom give credit where it belongs. Instead we are always ready with destructive criticism. I began to understand that this kind of criticism was my biggest obstacle.

Many of the Tibetan's explanations were strange to me at first, but I intuitively knew that at some later time I would understand what he meant. He used dreams as the means to help me see that the waking state is just another type of dream. He pointed out that I must be aware that dreams are the stuff of the mind, even dreams that frighten, in which monsters attack. And yet it is important to guard against such dreams by dealing with these monsters, precisely because they are produced by the mind. Dreams have a reality, just as daily life—which is also a dream—has a certain reality. To really comprehend what he was saying, my understanding of reality had to undergo a considerable change.

I was reminded of the exercise with the grain of rice and then of something that I had done myself when I was in my late twenties. I had seen a statue of the Buddha in an antique shop. It was not for sale, so I would go by the window and look at this Buddha again and again. It was so delicate, so beautiful, of such a fine nature that it had an almost ethereal quality. This image implanted itself so deeply in my mind that one day when I was in a strange mood and happened to be looking at the sky, suddenly this beautiful Buddha appeared in my mind's eye. I could see every detail.

Then came a moment when this image detached itself from my mind and was projected into the sky. The Buddha grew, it moved, it took on a life of its own. It became tremendous, it changed the position of its fingers and hands, occasionally the expression changed from inner serenity to smiling compassion. As this was happening, the image grew until it filled the sky completely.

Some portion of my mind seemed to be caught in it and another portion seemed not to be caught. One part of my mind became frightened enough to think of placing myself underneath the Buddha, whose lotus posture formed something like a roof under which I could move easily. It was as though I were taking refuge in the Buddha. My thoughts were, "If I go underneath and line up my spine with his, I will be all right." In my mind I moved "me" underneath the Buddha, and I lined up my spine with the spine of the Buddha. This brought a tremendous sense of well-being and security. It all happened so fast that I felt I had been moved at tremendous speed half way around the globe. I experienced indescribable bliss and ecstasy, which became a source of continuing strength and energy.

I began to understand that there was something in me that functioned beyond the everyday level. The exercises I learned from the Tibetan yogi were aimed at looking into the same unexplored level. The remembrance of this experience helped me to understand what he was saying to me.

It was as if the Buddha had made himself known to me, or I had contacted the Buddha-consciousness and was functioning under the patronage of the Buddha. Perhaps this kind of illusion helps us to understand that what we *think* is solid ground under our feet, is no more substantial than the imaginary worlds of our mind. Perhaps the importance of acquiring "supernatural powers," as they are called, is that it shows us that someone who has these abilities is no more supernatural than a genius in any other field. To use the term *spiritual genius* would perhaps help our understanding of saints and sages, without diminishing their value, or the reverence and adoration that we feel for them. It may allow us to see that we and they are part of the Oneness.

The Tibetan guru taught me how to visualize light. He taught me how to visualize light in various parts of my body. My hand should no longer be a hand, but a mass of dazzling light, so that I would be able to see the miracle of the hand. He had me look at a tree until my eyes were running, and burning with pain, and he would tell me that the tree was also a mass of light. Eventually I could see light around the tree. I did not see the tree itself as a mass of light, but I could see a beautiful aura of light around it.

He reminded me always to doubt. "If you don't doubt," he would say, "you can no longer learn. If you stop doubting, you stop breaking limitations."

I looked at him and said, "But I have taken all you have said very seriously, and I have followed your instructions implicitly. You don't mean to say I should doubt you?"

"Yes," he nodded his head.

I started to laugh. "Shall I doubt your very existence sitting in front of me?"

"Yes," he said, "that, too, is just an illusion."

The intermingling of the influences of the Tibetan guru and Swami Sivananda had a tremendous significance on my development. I see each of them as an expression of the divine mind. As long as we need concrete expressions of the divine mind, we draw on those souls who, in their great dedication and selflessness, allow themselves to be used, so that we can eventually learn to recognize the divine essence that is in all.

RESOURCES FOR THE READER

The "Tibetan Guru" left no writings, but the reader is referred to Swami Sivananda Radha's book, *Kundalini Yoga for the West,* which is highly influenced by the Tibetan's method and teachings.

Suggested Reading—Tibetan Yoga

EVANS-WENTZ, W. Y., ed. *Tibet's Great Yogi: Milarepa.* 2d ed. London: Oxford University Press, 1951.

LONGCHENPA. *Kindly Bent To Ease Us.* Translated by Herbert Guenther. Emeryville: Dharma Press, 1975.

SGAM.PO.PA *The Jewel Ornament of Liberation.* Translated by Herbert Guenther. London: Rider & Company, 1959.

CHAPTER 6

SAI BABA OF SHIRDI

Sai Baba of Shirdi, an Indian guru and healer who died in 1918, had a very peculiar way of introducing himself to me. This unusual introduction occurred before my second visit to India. My Canadian ashram was very young—just an ordinary house in Vancouver where eight of us lived permanently, though often as many as thirteen or fourteen people stayed for various reasons. Because everyone ate meals at the ashram, and the only car was used by those who worked, I had to walk to the food store usually several times a day, carrying back bags in both arms.

One day as I was returning from the store, a huge dog—almost the size of a bear, with very thick hair and an enormous head—started to walk behind me. Strangely enough, though I was usually afraid of large dogs, this one did not frighten me. He followed me closely, walked with me through the garden gate, up the steps to the porch, and then into the house. "You poor fellow," I said, "you must be either very hungry or thirsty." So I offered him first water, then milk, and then food. But the dog wasn't interested in any of it.

This particular day I had to return to the store several times, and the dog followed me there and back each time. By the second trip, I had already left the door open for him. After putting the food away, I went upstairs to my room to take a few moments rest. The dog again followed me and then remained in my room while I went down to cook dinner. With seven young men coming home from hard physical work, I made sure their food was ready on time to avoid flaring tempers. (Since I was the only woman in the house and this was the 1950s, I was expected to do all the housework and cooking, all the shopping, and all the laundry, which also meant carrying it back and forth to the laundromat by hand.)

What could I say to the others about this enormous dog? I didn't want him to be put out at night, where he could be chased away or harmed on the streets, so I kept absolutely quiet about him, and he, in turn, stayed quietly in my room. After satsang the dog changed his position to lie against the door, and because he was quite heavy, I was ensured of uninterrupted quiet time. The next morning when I went downstairs, the dog followed me. He stayed with me in this way for three days and nights. What was unusual was that he never ate, and he drank only a little water. He seemed content just to keep me company.

On the fourth day, I was in the garden with him when he quietly wandered off, without my noticing. Because I had come to really like him, I searched the streets, asking people if they had seen such a dog or if they knew of anyone who had one or had lost one. But as mysteriously as he had appeared, this dog also disappeared.

The next time the dog came into my mind was in 1959, when I had returned to India. We were all very happily gathered together on the sunroof of an ashram building when I saw a huge dog walk by. I eagerly asked the nearest swami, "What kind of dog is that? Where do these dogs come from? Have they been exported to America?"

He told me that such dogs were used by the hill tribes to protect their cattle from wild animals. As I continued to ask questions, he started to get annoyed. "Why do you ask all this?"

I said that I had never seen a similar dog anywhere in Europe or Canada, except once. Then I told him the whole story of my experience with the very friendly dog there, who seemed to be of this type.

Sai Baba of Shirdi: "He was the only teacher I had heard of who was at home in both Islam and Hinduism, and was able to use the teachings of both."

Suddenly all the swamis burst out laughing, as if I had made the greatest joke in the world. When asked what they found so funny they said, "That *dog* you're talking about was Sai Baba."

"Who's Sai Baba?" I asked, having never heard of him.

They said that Sai Baba was a saint who had lived in the tiny village of Shirdi, but had powers of projecting himself to different places. He would sometimes get acquainted with those he might or might not accept, by taking the form of just such a large dog. "This," said one of the swamis, "was one of his peculiar tests to find out how kind-hearted you are. How do you treat animals?"

I sighed with relief at having nothing to regret in my way of treating this huge dog. Was it Sai Baba? I have never found out for sure.

But years later I was delighted when I was given a film on Sai Baba, which contained a confirmation of Sai Baba's ability to project himself in this way. In the film, one woman asked Sai Baba, "Won't you come to my house for dinner?"

Sai Baba said, "Yes, yes, I am coming, I am surely coming."

She waited and waited and waited. Then a dog came along and tried to eat the food. The woman chased the dog away because the food was meant for Sai Baba.

In the evening at Sai Baba's satsang she complained that he hadn't come. He said, "What do you want? I was there and you chased me away."

She said, "What I chased away was a dog—I didn't want the dog to eat your food."

"No, no," Sai Baba said, "it was me."

Many of the stories that the swamis told me in 1959, I rediscovered later in books about Sai Baba. Some of the stories of his life and teachings made a deep impression on me. He was the only teacher I had heard of who was at home in both Islam and Hinduism, and was able to use the teachings of both. For him there was no difference because he taught by symbol and metaphor.

Sai Baba did not ask his disciples to practice mantras, to read scriptures, or to recite *sutras.*[1] People often thought he must be an easy guru to follow, but what they did not realize was how much surrender and obedience he demanded, as the following incident shows:

A man and his wife came to Sai Baba with their sick child, hoping for a cure. Sai Baba said he would do his best to restore the daughter to good health but told the man, "I want you to be here for the next three days."

By the first night, the child seemed very well indeed. The man started thinking to himself, "My tonga," (which is like a horse and buggy taxi), "is still here. How will I find another tonga in this village in the wilderness to return to Bombay? And why should I pay this tonga driver

---

[1] Sutras are aphorisms that encapsulate doctrines.

"I often have the sense of something of Sai Baba's spirit, like the spirit of all great saintly people, is protecting the earth from total disintegration."

for three days when I'm not even using it? Anyway, I can't do anything here except wait."

The man felt that his reasoning was quite logical, so against Sai Baba's instructions, he decided they should leave that same night.

The tonga driver made very slow headway and in the middle of the night, in the darkest forest, the tonga broke down. Of course the man was now very afraid of robbers. When he heard someone calling, he became even more frightened for himself and his family. Finally the person who was calling came close enough that he could hear his own name. In the moonlight he recognized one of the residents from Sai Baba's ashram, who said, "Sai Baba wants you to come back immediately."

"How did he know that this tonga was broken down?"

He said, "You better ask him that yourself."

When the man got back to the ashram, Sai Baba simply said to him, "Never again act against the orders I give you."

With our Western upbringing and education, we often have great difficulties understanding the law of karma, and think of it as punishment. To accept challenges as an opportunity to further our development comes much later in our understanding. The following accounts of Sai Baba are helpful in trying to understand this aspect of karma:

A baby died soon after birth and the parents were grief-stricken. One of Sai Baba's women disciples who was trying to comfort the parents asked Sai Baba,

"But why would the child die?"

"Sometimes," Sai Baba said, "the soul can enter life and then realize that it cannot accomplish its purpose for taking birth. The child left and went to circumstances that would better support the purpose for incarnating again."

We understand very little of our own minds, and of the force in us that we call "soul." Each of us has a purpose to fulfill in life, even if we do not always perceive it. To develop the consciousness necessary to be in communion with the Most High is not an easy task.

Another story is told of a father who brought his sick little daughter to Sai Baba hoping he would cure her. But Sai Baba said, "I know why you have come and it is not right. I cannot help you. The girl is of divine nature and her life on earth will be very short. It would be best if you could stay home and spend as much time with her as you can, instead of going to work, because otherwise you may not see her again."

If the girl had a divine nature and would die soon, what was her purpose on earth? The answer would depend on what influence the child had on those she lived with. She could have sanctified her parents. She could have come to repay the parents for their goodness in previous lives. Her short life may have been to teach her parents that love in separation is different from love in union. In separation we become more aware. Love is freed of possessiveness and personal gratification, so each individual learns to be more giving. Human nature, which always seeks some immediate tangible reward, is also rewarded by separation, but it takes humility to wait in the state of receptivity needed to receive that reward.

The following story of Sai Baba explains another aspect of karma—the responsibility one must be willing to take to help another.

A father fell ill. His high fever caused his son a lot of worry. The father gave his son 500 rupees and told him to travel to Sai Baba and donate the money to him, to be used as he wished. On receiving it, Baba began to shiver with fever. A devotee, worrying about him, asked why he would take on the illness.

"When we do anything for others," Sai Baba answered, "we have to take on the burden and responsibility ourselves."

Soon after this, the father recovered, though he may not have understood the great gift of karmic release Sai Baba had given him.

This confirmed a situation I had experienced with my own guru, Swami Sivananda. He was approached by a man who asked him, "Can you save my wife's life? I have five children. The doctor said it's hopeless, and that he can do nothing."

I was present at the time and was shocked when Swami Sivananda said, almost as if he were disgusted, "Get up and go home! Take care of her! What are you doing here?"

The man was shattered. He left. But a few days later a telegram arrived saying that upon his return home, he had found that his wife was better.

I told Sivananda that I had been disturbed when he was so rough with the man. He explained, "Oh, you see, if I had not been, then he would have thanked me instead of the Divine."

Another of Sai Baba's teachings provided great release for me from one of my troubling personal concerns.

At Sivananda Ashram in India I had witnessed how some devotees threw down their malas and ocher robes in great anger, and stomped out of the ashram. I could not understand why anyone would leave Swami Sivananda. Even if he was not a saint by their standards, it was obvious even to me, a newcomer, that he was a man of great character. When I visited Papa Ramdas at his ashram, I encountered the same issue. I could not understand why only one swami had remained there more than ten years. Of all the disciples over the years, he was the only one left. I did not dare to ask Papa Ramdas the reason for this. Later on, when Yasodhara Ashram[2] came into existence in Canada, I had to experience the same thing. People were coming, people were going. Was it my fault? Was my mind not clear enough, pure enough? Was my dedication not complete? What was the reason for this? Sai Baba gave me the answer through one of his stories:

One day a devotee, seeing a crowd around Sai Baba, asked whether all of them derived benefit. For his reply, Sai Baba pointed to a flowering mango tree and to the many blossoms on the ground. He replied, "Is it the tree's fault that only a few will turn into fruit?"

This relieved me of the worry that my mistakes caused people to leave. Yes, there are many flowers falling to the ground. Is it the fault of the tree? Or is it that some people can take only a little of the unadulterated teachings?

Sai Baba left a last message:

One of his devotees asked him one day, "Baba, I have bought the property next to your mosque, because I want to build a temple dedicated to Krishna. Will you bless the temple?"

Sai Baba said, "Oh, not only will I bless it, I will stay in it."

The man hurried to have the temple finished soon because Sai Baba said he would stay there. What greater honor, what greater

---

[2] Yasodhara Ashram is an ashram founded by Swami Radha in 1956 in British Columbia, Canada.

blessing—for him, for the family, for anybody who would come to the temple dedicated to Krishna!

What he never anticipated was that Sai Baba would order the preparation of his *samadhi,*[3] in the temple.

Before he died Sai Baba promised not only this man, but all people, "If you come to the temple with sincerity and purity of heart and mind, I will always grant you your wish, if you ask me."

I have certainly felt the blessings of Sai Baba in my own life. Though I have never met him in human form nor had the privilege of visiting his temple in Shirdi, I have definitely been touched by the spirit of his teachings. I often have the sense that something of Sai Baba's spirit, like the spirit of all great saintly people, is protecting the earth from total disintegration.

RESOURCES FOR THE READER

Suggested Reading

MURTHY, T. S. ANANTHA. *Life and Teachings of Sri Sai Baba of Shirdi.* Malleswaram, Bangalore, 1974.

OSBORNE, ARTHUR. *The Incredible Sai Baba.* London: Rider & Company, 1957.

SAHUKAR, MANI. *Sai Baba: The Saint of Shirdi.* Bombay: Somaiya Publications, 1971.

Videotape

Shirdi Ke Sai Baba. Copyright Superstar Video Ltd. Distributed through M.K. Enterprises Ltd., 5509 16th Ave. S., Seattle, WA 98108

---

[3] The place where he would be buried.

CHAPTER 7

PAPA RAMDAS

I met Swami Ramdas,[1] who likes to be known as "Papa," on my second visit to India, at Swami Sivananda's suggestion. Disciples of the two gurus often visited each other's ashram, since there was great affection and respect between the two men. I was eager to see Papa Ramdas because, although I had never actually met him in person, I had nevertheless encountered him before.

Three years earlier, when I was wearing the orange robe as my guru had requested, I gave a public lecture in Vancouver. In the audience there was a couple who had been in correspondence with Swami Sivananda for about six years and had always hoped that someday they would have enough money to go to India and meet him. Now they were overjoyed to be in personal contact with one of his initiated disciples, and immediately invited me to their beautiful home.

[1] Although he was not a sanyasi, Ramdas was called "Swami" as a sign of respect, in much the same way that Gandhi was given the title "Mahatma."

"The world took on a new light in the company of Papa Ramdas. . . . He seemed to lift the heaviness and free the joy."

They must have been puzzled over how to treat me—what sort of things would I eat? They were very excited and anxious to do the right thing. When I arrived I saw that the table was set with the best silver and dishes, on a tablecloth that was hand-embroidered.

My hostess offered me a seat facing the window so that I could look out while they made final preparations for the meal. Over the muted clatter of the pots, pans, and dishes, I heard them whispering in the kitchen. I may have waited fifteen minutes or it may have been half an hour. Because Swami Sivananda discouraged idleness, I had learned not to let my mind drift, and so I began to do the only spiritual practice that was suitable under the circumstances. I looked into the sky and repeated a mantra silently to myself. This certainly would contribute to a harmonious spiritual atmosphere, and I had also been told that it would leave some of the power of the mantra behind. I remembered Gurudev's instructions to accept any invitation, even to homes I might not like, because the power of the mantra would benefit those who lived there. Perhaps his instructions were meant to help me accept all people, especially those with whom I might otherwise have had little contact.

Suddenly there appeared in the sky a big picture like an oversized portrait. I recognized it immediately as Paramahansa Yogananda, with his long curly hair and penetrating dark eyes, just as he is shown on the covers of the books I had seen. At first I thought my mind was playing tricks, and while I was wondering how the mind did that, the image faded and another, which I could not identify, appeared in the sky. It was the round face of a man who was aged, toothless, and bald. At first I thought it must be Gandhi, but realized I was mistaken because although the glasses were there, the ears did not protrude as Gandhi's so typically did. It was a smiling face expressing kindness and love. And while I was wondering who it was, the couple came in with dinner.

I asked them if they knew of Yogananda, and they said they were aware of him, and had read his books and teachings. Then I asked them if there was any other saint or person of a saintly nature they were involved with, and they said the only other person was Swami Sivananda, my guru. So I kept my experience to myself.

Many months later I was invited to Vancouver again to show some slides and give a talk. Just before I returned to Montreal, there was a long-distance phone call asking me to stop in Ottawa on my way home. When I arrived in Ottawa, I was met at the airport by a very warm and friendly lady. She told me she had been studying yoga for a number of years, and had been in contact with the authors of many yogic books.

Suddenly she turned to me and said, "I hope you don't mind, but I cannot accept your guru for myself. I already have a guru."

I smiled and answered, "That's quite all right. In any case, in their hearts the gurus are one."

When we reached her house and had settled in her living room with a cup of tea, she immediately got out a book to show me the picture of her guru. There he was, the man that I had seen in the sky!

The lady told me that his name was Ramdas. She was only too happy to give me the book, and of course I accepted her gift eagerly so that I could find out more about this man. Again I kept my experience to myself because I was shy, and fearful that it would not be believed, and I did not want to cheapen it by talking about it.

So now back in India I was most happy to write to Ramdas at Ananda Ashram, as Gurudev suggested. I received a very quick reply inviting me to come for two weeks.

I had phoned ahead to find out how to get to the ashram, and was told that I should take a taxi. Since they knew when to expect me, Papa was standing at the flight of steps leading to the ashram when I arrived. I rushed to him almost like a child coming home, taking his hands and looking into his smiling eyes, because I felt that I had already met him that day in the sky. I was not sure if Papa was embarrassed by such a welcome at the first meeting, so I was greatly relieved when he helped me over my uncertainty and said, "So we meet again. Now you are here, Radha."

The devotees who were standing around said, "Oh, you have been here before?"

I shook my head.

"Then you must have met Papa when he was in America?"

"No, that was not how it happened."

With a sweet smile Papa said, "You can all come to my room at two o'clock and I will give permission for Radha to tell the story of our meeting."

We gathered at the time he had arranged for us and I told my story. There was silence for a few minutes. Finally one of the ladies asked, "Papa, why did the other people not see you? Is it because Radha is so holy?"

Papa replied, "This has nothing to do with holiness. It is rather like a message being delivered to the one who should receive it and sometimes this is the only way the message can be given."

Another woman said, "I don't understand what the message was."

"Ramdas liked to hold court under a banyan tree. He talked of God as a Supreme Being, and even though I did not share his concept, Papa was so inspiring that while he talked I simply forgot the discomfort that the fleas inflicted."

Ramdas answered, "Swami Sivananda is Radha's guru, and he and I often meet in the heart." With that, Ramdas pointed to a picture of Sivananda that was on the wall. "She could not meet him without eventually meeting me also. So that is the clue." He turned to me. "Sivanandaji recognized that you must meet me, and so he sent you. You couldn't meet one without the other."

These remarks clarified for me the way to discriminate between a genuine experience and a creation of the mind. Even if my visit to Papa had not given me more, this alone would have made it very valuable.

Later in the afternoon he spoke about one of his disciples who was now at Sivananda Ashram because his family had tried to persuade him to give up spiritual life. The mother had dreams that her son would become a successful doctor or lawyer, and she was quite upset that he had chosen to become a sanyasi. So Ramdas had arranged for him to spend some time at Sivananda Ashram in order to escape pressure from his parents. For me this was another example of the closeness of the two ashrams.

As I had seen in Vancouver, Papa had a round head, he wore glasses, and had no teeth. He kept his dentures in a little bag and used them only when eating. Without any embarrassment he would put his teeth in or take them out, regardless of who happened to be around. He suffered from diabetes, which is very widespread in India, and had to have daily injections. Holiness or saintliness does not seem to depend on a healthy body. Vivekananda, the great disciple of Ramakrishna, died quite young of diabetes, and my own guru was also a diabetic. Ramdas would not explain his illness as taking on his disciples' karma, as many other Indians do. He accepted it as his own.

After I had told my story, I went to the room I had been given. There was a big four-poster bed and, as at Sivananda Ashram, the bathroom had a tank about two feet high that was filled from a cistern. The water for the cistern was carried by bucket from the well, just as it was in biblical times. For washing, you poured the water over your body with a small pitcher. Sanitary facilities were there in simple Indian style, but luxuries like toilet paper were missing. One day I saw a snake as thick as my wrist, in the cistern, and wondered if it was poisoning the water.

That evening I was plagued by bugs different from the bedbugs that had bothered me so much at Sivananda Ashram. There were many mosquitoes, and fleas so tiny they were almost invisible. At about two o'clock in the morning someone knocked on my door and brought in nets to put over the bed for protection from the mosquitoes. Papa had awakened and had wondered if I was well looked after and if the mosquito nets had been put up. When he discovered this had not been done, he knew that I could not possibly be asleep, so he sent someone to help me. I was most grateful for this confirmation of Papa's thoughtfulness.

That took care of the mosquitoes, but the fleas were in the woollen carpets that had been put down on the concrete floors, and the net did not keep them out. Different parts of India make life uncomfortable in different ways. The fleas continued to bother me. I found myself in an unpleasant dilemma: I was being bitten in every part of me, yet I hesitated to say anything in case it would be interpreted as criticism.

However, during the morning meditation with Papa, which took place at five o'clock, my squirming drew his attention. He asked me why I was so restless. I told him my body was itching all over and I didn't know what to do about it. I was not yet able to put my mind into the itch to go beyond it. There were just too many bites and new ones

"During the morning meditation with Papa, which took place at five o'clock, my squirming drew his attention... I was not yet able to put my mind into the itch and go beyond it."

continually coming up. Papa said this would be taken care of, and later somebody brought me an American repellent spray that helped greatly.

Ramdas liked to hold court under a banyan tree. It was a good time of year for this, with enough shade, enough warmth, and enough breeze from the ocean, which one could see from the hilltop glistening in the distance. He talked of God as a Supreme Being, and even though I did not share his concept, Papa was so inspiring that while he talked I simply forgot the discomfort that the fleas inflicted.

But at other times I continued to be troubled by the bugs and did not dare to kill them, knowing that Indians do not believe in killing. When I asked Papa about this, his answer was most practical. He said, "If God in the form of a thief breaks into your house, you call God in the form of the policeman to take the thief away."

"But the divine power and holiness of this place should protect it so a thief would not come—or would just be deflected," I remarked.

"That could happen," Papa said, "but it is not right always to ask for divine intervention that way."

I turned my questioning to the subject of rats and asked if he had many visits from them, since they seemed to be so common everywhere.

He answered that with rats it is not so easy. "We used to tell the king of the rats not to come onto our territory, and that worked. But then they went to the neighbors who killed them. So maybe we just put the responsibility onto the neighbors."

I wanted to have his answer to my question really clear. I asked, "What do you do about rats at the ashram now?"

"We trap them," Papa confirmed, "and they are killed."

One day two ladies arrived and joined Papa's gathering. One of them felt as if she were in the presence of God, and she was crying softly but happily, like someone who had come home after a long absence. The other lady felt that she was in the presence of the devil. She pulled at the sleeve of her companion and said, "Let's get out of here. Just look at him."

When she got no response, she left, alone. I followed her outside and she asked me about her friend's reaction to Ramdas.

"It depends what you open yourself to," I answered. "Your friend opened herself to something good, something holy, and that is what she found and responded to in Ramdas."

Perhaps Ramdas's presence made this lady uncomfortable because for the first time she could see the depths of her emotional garbage, and so her own negativity prevented her from responding to his holiness. During the meditation that followed I could not help but think about the contrast of their differences in perceptions. I realized how important it is to pay attention to what you open yourself up to, and to let in only the Light.

At another time I asked Ramdas how he dealt with the ups and downs, the fickleness of the mind that one day accepts and the next day rejects. "Do you ever have such troubles—when one day you would take all that the world can give, and the next you want only to go back to your heavenly home?"

He said that he understood very well indeed. "Do you know what I would do? I would tell God that he must hold onto me, because he must know that I cannot hold on to him." Perhaps under those circumstances, personifying the God-Force is the only way to handle such moments. I decided that this was a good example to follow, even though my ideas about God were foggy. I have often made the same request and I owe much to that for having guided me through many troubles and tribulations. Some of these came out of my own nature, and some were projected onto me by those I met. In the beginning I did not have the discrimination to distinguish between the two.

I had prepared numerous questions for Papa before coming to his ashram, and I had armed myself with a tape recorder, packing my luggage with as many small reels as I could. There were certain questions that Papa would not answer until the tape was finished. That irritated me because I worried that I would not remember all his answers well enough on my own. Finally, one day I had enough courage to ask him why some things could not be put on tape.

He said, "The temptation for you will be to let others listen to the tape. Then you would be responsible for the listeners getting information that they would not be able to grasp and this might pull the rug out from under their feet. You must listen with your heart, with your inner ear, and it is only the final answer that you won't have on the tape. Everything that leads up to it is there, and I know you will not forget the rest."

One day he asked me if I had pictures of Canada. I had a few photographs and some slides, which he wanted me to show to the people at the ashram. As I showed them, he interjected his own experiences in America. Among the slides was one that showed the altar I had in Montreal before I first came to India. It had a picture of my guru and a cross, along with some candles.

Papa looked at it and said, "Why is the cross so small? I thought Christians had huge crosses."

I told him that this was a piece of jewelry cut from black onyx, with some pearls in the center and gold around the edge, such as a bishop might wear. I had it on my altar because I intended to bring it to Swami Sivananda as a spiritual gift, and from the moment I purchased it until I left for India, I kept it beside his picture.

"Atcha, atcha," said Ramdas, with the particularly Indian gesture, moving his head from side to side in much the same way that a Westerner says no. "You bought this *before* you came to India?"

"Yes, Papa."

I told him that I had first bought a small cross, but when I saw pictures of Gurudev and saw what a huge man he was, I realized it was not big enough for him. I searched the city until I found this one. The strange thing was that, when I first saw it I could not afford it. But the week before I left, the price was reduced by $100, and that made it possible for me to buy it.

Then Papa said, with the wistful smile that I had learned to love and from which I had come to expect something extraordinary, "So you brought your own message to Sivanandaji." He pointed to the picture of Gurudev that hung above the door.

"I don't understand, Papa."

He explained, "The symbolic message is in the cross. And now I can understand why you got the name Radha."

Referring to the black onyx of the cross, he said, "Black is the favorite color of Radha who searches for the Most High in the form of Krishna. Although she had a vision of him, still she knew that she could never know all of him. Black is symbolic of the unknown. The pearls symbolize the intensity of her search, her desire to be one with the Lord. Tears that she sheds with a sincere, deep longing for the Divine turn into pearls that Radha strings into a mala. The gold edges of the cross indicate preciousness, and the purity of her search."

I looked at Papa in great bewilderment, "I still don't understand."

So he elaborated a little more, saying, "Gold appears when all the impurities have been burned away. You were attracted to this cross as a gift for your guru, so indirectly you told him what you wanted. Therefore he gave you the name in memory of Radha. Because of the teachings and stories of Radha and Krishna, Sivanandaji recognized the purpose of your coming.

"The pearls of the cross will have told him that whatever work he does with you, whatever knowledge he imparts, will not be in vain. According to the story, Lord Krishna had asked Radha for a pearl from her mala because he wanted to grow a pearl tree. Although Radha could not believe that one could grow a tree from a pearl, she sent the whole mala to the Lord, rather than ruin it by removing a bead. One day," Papa said, obviously delighted to tell the story, "the messenger returned and took her to Lord Krishna, who showed her the pearl tree he had grown from the pearl he had taken from her mala."

At that moment this sounded like a beautiful fairy tale, but I still did not understand what he was trying to tell me.

"These pearls on the cross are an expression of your own sincerity. One day you will grow your own pearl tree."

"I don't understand." I was becoming almost desperate and felt terribly inadequate, if not stupid. I must have had a puzzled and helpless

Papa Ramdas and Mother Krishna Bai. "Because of the relationship between them over the years, the villagers learned to regard Mother Krishna Bai as equal to Ramdas. He himself has stated that she has the same level of consciousness that he has."

look on my face because Ramdas continued the explanation, finally realizing that the cultural differences prevented my understanding.

"You will inspire many people who in turn will inspire many other people, and this is how a tree bears fruit. But this is a special fruit. The fruit is the longing for the Lord, for Lord Krishna."

Later when I was sitting by a well, looking at the surface of the water, I was able to come in touch with the stillness of my mind, and I understood what Papa had said.

This was different from the symbolism in the paintings and diagrams of the Kundalini system and it was more than just a story with a moral. This was more difficult for me to grasp, but I understood that it did more than just point the way for the seeker.

The world took on a new light in the company of Papa Ramdas, and the forces within, which I had considered terribly difficult to deal with and sometimes depressing, I could now see in a different color. He seemed to lift the heaviness and free the joy.

Later in my visit Papa told me some of the history of the ashram, and how for twenty years he and Mother Krishna Bai had struggled. First they had cooked for everybody, but people had complained about the food. Then he built houses so they could cook their own, and still people complained: the houses were too small or not to their liking. Then Papa Ramdas and Mother Krishna Bai decided that everyone who worked for the ashram would be given a house, but they would all take turns cooking and would eat together. When this did not prove to be a harmonious arrangement, all houses except one for the manager and his family were turned into guest facilities, and everyone else had to find living quarters outside the ashram. Then they received a moderate wage from Mother Krishna Bai for their work.

Who was Mother Krishna Bai? She had given up her family, her husband and children, to follow Ramdas. And the villagers who venerated him as a saint were angry, jealous, and worried that this very beautiful woman would rob him of his saintliness by making herself a temptation. They had underestimated Ramdas's sincerity and strength, but also the sincerity of Mother Krishna Bai's search. She still bears scars from stones that villagers had thrown at her to keep her away. Often she had to hide. Insults were heaped on her, and although she was a very accomplished woman, in the eyes of the villagers she was nothing more than an unfaithful wife. But because of the relationship between them, over the years the villagers learned to regard Mother Krishna Bai as an equal to Ramdas. He himself has stated that she has the same level of consciousness that he has. He felt that it had been in God's plan to show that a man and a woman could overcome any obstacles created by sex on the spiritual path.

Theirs was a work of combined labor. And perhaps because there was a woman at Ananda Ashram it ran very smoothly. Everything was orderly, well-organized, and clean.

Everybody has to work at Papa's ashram. Mother Krishna Bai looks after the affairs of the ashram, taking much of the load off Papa's shoulders, and seeing to it that the work is done. She does not speak English but her actions spoke to me. Papa was willing to translate for me and tell me anything I wanted to know about her. He pointed out that, as well as having a high state of consciousness, the Mother was very practical, and when she took ashram affairs into her hands Papa was wise enough not to interfere with the changes she made.

While I was there Mataji refused to allow an Indian sadhu to stay longer than the customary three days, because he was a troublemaker. At a gathering under the big banyan tree, the sadhu approached Papa and asked his permission to stay. Papa looked at him sternly and asked if he had talked to Mataji. The sadhu had to admit that he had, and that she had refused. Then, for the first time, I heard Papa speak with a ring of anger in his voice: "How dare you come to me behind her back?" He ordered him to leave at once. Ramdas would never go against Mataji's decisions, which was why there was harmony at the ashram. He did not put himself any higher than her. He could not say that she had as high a state of consciousness as himself without giving her that same authority.

Visitors had to give two hours of their time daily to the work of the ashram as an expression of appreciation for its purpose. There was a vegetable garden, and cows that needed to be milked and looked after. Because I had no experience with cows, I was assigned to the garden. However, after a few days the gardener realized that I was not well. I had a fever, but I did not want to mention it and have it interpreted as an excuse for avoiding work, and I did want to show my appreciation through the work. But when Mataji was told, she gave orders that I should rest.

Papa had been a graduate engineer before he renounced. He had received a mantra initiation from his father, but had never been initiated into sanyas. However, he lived the life of a renunciate and he told me stories of his years of *tapas*[2] when he dwindled to the size of a skeleton.

---

[2] A tapas is a concentrated discipline and austerity; a burning, flaming devotion to attaining the spiritual goal

Having the name Ramdas indicates that he worshipped God in the form of Ram, and he maintained an incredible childlike faith that Ram would look after him. He would go in search of food at strange hours when wild beasts were prowling about, and he would say to Ram, "Show your devotee how you will get him safely back to his little hut." When he was unable to find food, he would say, "Let us see how you will feed your devotee. You cannot just let him starve to death before giving him the vision of you." Again and again his incredible faith was rewarded.

When I first met Papa Ramdas he was so skinny you could count his ribs, but the next time I saw him he had a potbelly. I asked him why he had gotten fat, and he explained that earlier he had asked Ram to nourish him, but when he was sure that he would be looked after, he began to eat normally.

One time Papa was traveling on a train in the days when sadhus could do so without paying. People had gathered to see him off, and someone had given him a kilo bag of sweets. Ramdas tried to share them with everyone and long after that small bag should have been empty, he was still handing them out. That reminded me of the story of Jesus with the loaves and fishes.

Although the stories of his experiences were so real and conveyed something of the spirit that filled him, they also created a feeling of sadness in me. It was like taking a nostalgic look back at childhood. The same kind of childlike faith had brought me to India and had carried me to this point. But it seemed to me that with my different background and culture, I also had to use my reason and intellect. I could not shut them off. I saw myself struggling to create a bridge between reason and faith.

I had thought that I would have a last important spiritual question to ask Ramdas; instead I used the opportunity to find out how he handled the administrative side of the ashram. What were the problems with people? There were many.

I asked Papa, "Where are the disciples who were with you when you started?"

He said that only one had stayed, a young man in an orange robe who had been with him for ten years. The manager, who drew a salary, had also been here from the beginning. Where were all the others? This was a question that worried me a great deal. Would I be responsible for those who left our ashram in the West? Would it be my fault? This was the topic of the longest discussion I had with Papa.

"People today are restless," he said. "There are more good teachers than there are students. Do not worry. Let people go if the accumulation of their good karma has been exhausted. Others will come. In the literature of the past, the gurus also complained that there were only a handful among their many disciples who had the sincerity and stamina to follow the path to Higher Consciousness."

The two weeks of my stay had gone so fast, and when the time came to leave, I voiced my regret to Ramdas that I had to go. Immediately he said, "No, no, you can't go." Then he asked, "Is there something not quite right?"

I told Papa that when the manager had accepted payment for my room and board for these two weeks, he mentioned that this was the longest Papa allowed anyone to stay. So I had made my travel arrangements.

"I've had a wonderful time," I said, "but you allow people to stay only two weeks."

With a wistful smile on his face, he said, "That is a safeguard for those who bring trouble."

Obviously I had not given him any trouble; when there is respect, love, and devotion, there is no time or place for trouble. Now I regretted not having told him of my nearing departure. It had not occurred to me that I would be welcome enough in his ashram that he would allow me to stay longer than the general rule. However, I could not change my plans because I was now expected at Sivananda Ashram and Papa knew I could not disappoint Sivananda.

Then Papa gave instructions to the manager to give me the names and addresses of all his American devotees so that I could contact them and share the pictures I had taken, and tell of my joyous visit with him and Mother Krishna Bai at Ananda Ashram.

Dear old Papa Ramdas left his body in 1963, in the same month and year as Gurudev Sivananda. Mother Krishna Bai carries on the work of the ashram. I have often thought of his saying that it is good to recognize our weaknesses, but we also have to look for the strength to support ourselves. Through his childlike faith Ramdas showed the direction in which it could be found.

RESOURCES FOR THE READER

Suggested Reading

RAMDAS, SWAMI. *Gita Sandesh (Message of the Gita).* 4th ed. Kanhangad: Anandashram, 1950.

RAMDAS, SWAMI. *In Quest of God.* 5th ed. Kanhangad: Anandashram, 1946.
RAMDAS, SWAMI. *In the Vision of God.* 3d ed. Kanhangad: Anandashram, 1950.
RAMDAS, SWAMI. *World is God.* Kanhangad: Anandashram, 1955.

Ramdas Center

Anandashram, P.O. Anandashram, Via Kanhangad, South India.

CHAPTER 8

DILIP KUMAR ROY AND INDIRA DEVI

Mail delivery must be a problem all over the world, so I could not be disturbed when Dilip Kumar Roy and Indira Devi did not receive and respond to the letters I had sent from Canada announcing my arrival. Because I had no reply from them, I did not know that they had changed their location. Fortunately, when I got to Poona I found that they were still in the same part of the city but had moved a little further along the street. Although they are well known and revered in America, here in their own country the taxi driver did not know who I was looking for, and even their immediate neighbors knew nothing about them.

Much of the background of Dilip Kumar Roy and Indira Devi can be found in their delightful and inspiring book, *Pilgrims of the Stars.* In Germany and England, where Dilip studied music, he moved in the highest intellectual circles and enjoyed the friendship of philosophers as well as musicians. However, he turned his back on this type of life when he became a disciple of Sri Aurobindo. Indira Devi, his daughter disciple, had

Dilip Kumar Roy speaks with Swami Radha about the path of devotion. "He regretted that for so many years he had been ruled by his intellect, but now he knew that he must give his heart an equal place."

left her family, home, and children to answer the inner call, which brought her to Dilip in her search for the Divine. I was aware of how similar the fate of Indira Devi was to that of Mother Krishna Bai.

Indira showed a respectful humility and devotion to Dada, as she lovingly called Dilip. At satsang she was seated next to him in a place set a little higher than the rest of the room, and served as a focal point for the wandering mind. Dilip would play a few chords and ragas, and then begin to sing. Even though he was in his sixties, his voice had a very sweet quality. It called to the earnest seeker, drawing out beautiful feelings of devotion, and striking a chord in the heart of the listener. Indira lightly tapped cymbals together in time with the music, and gently rocked back and forth with her eyes closed. In a while the sound of the cymbals ceased and then even her gentle rocking stopped. Indira had entered a different world where her soul and Dilip's merged into one.

After satsang Dilip addressed me, saying that if I wanted brilliant sparks of intellect, clever argumentation and philosophizing, I had come to the wrong person because today he knew better. The path he

Indira Devi and Dilip Kumar Roy at evening satsang, with Swami Radha in attendance. "In her meditations Indira hears the songs of Mira, the Beggar Princess who lived in the sixteenth century and gave up her royal position to become a mendicant in the service of Lord Krishna."

followed was that of devotion. "Reason and logic will not take anyone to higher levels of consciousness," he said.

To hear this from a man who had such qualifications in education and such intellectual capability was reassuring. He spoke of the many scholars who study scriptures and spiritual texts and can speak eloquently, but do not really understand what they are saying. They cannot grasp the depths of their subject because they are infatuated with their own intellects. These pundits, anxious to display their intelligence, engage in mental gymnastics, with disagreements resulting in clashes of egos.

Later Dilip and Indira inquired where I was staying. They were very surprised that they had not received my letters, and so had no room to offer me in their house because they had already given hospitality to a number of people. They suggested a hotel where they felt I would be safe and where the owner was honest. I was invited to come back every day if I wished, and I did this for two weeks. We had many interesting conversations in which we talked about devotion as the antidote for all manifestations of the ego. Dilip had spent some time with the Ramakrishna Order, and understood that it was their devotion that had made them such outstanding people. He

Indira Devi in front of the shrine where Swami Radha witnessed the miraculous incident of Krishna accepting Indira's offering of food.

regretted that for so many years he had been ruled by his intellect, but now he knew that he must give his heart an equal place.

Indira, as hostess and mother of the house, was extremely busy preparing food for the many visitors. She had to simplify the meals greatly to be able to look after everyone and still maintain her schedule of spiritual practice and meditation. Before each meal she would go to the altar at the end of the hall, and offer the food first to Lord Krishna, expressing her devotion to him. Everyone would wait until the offering had been made before the meal would begin.

One day she came to Dilip in tears, saying, "Dada, Lord Krishna won't come to bless the food. Do you think it is too simple for him?"

Dilip told her that she would have to tell Lord Krishna that if he expected her to cook for all his devotees and continue her practices to honor him, that he would have to accept her offering of the simple foods. "Tell him that you cannot take the time from worshipping him."

Indira seemed to be quickly pacified. She was truly Krishna's child.

She went back into the other room, which was their bhajan hall, and as Dilip had suggested she began once again to intone Lord Krishna's name in prayer. Soon, miraculously, there were the marks of fingers scooping up food and I could hear the sound of someone licking his hands. After that, dinner was served, because Indira knew that Lord Krishna had come to bless the food.

The sophisticated Westerner might demand a rational explanation. I saw it happen and I cannot give one. Perhaps this aspect of the Divine that Indira worshipped so devotedly as Lord Krishna, used her mind as a tool. I can only say that her devotion expressed a quality of absolute sincerity. But this is not something that could be investigated by another mind, however brilliant or scientifically trained. There has to be a respect for Creative Energy when it manifests in a way that inspires and leads us to contemplate the profound mystery of life. Even those who cannot accept divine intervention must ask, Is it not creativity of the highest order when we are uplifted to a new understanding of the potential that lies within us?

Indira is Bengali and she does not understand Hindi. Yet in her meditations she hears the songs of Mira, the Beggar Princess[1] who lived in the sixteenth century and gave up her royal position to become a mendicant in the service of Lord Krishna. Indira does not speak the language in which Mira sang, nor is she very musical, yet she would bring back the lyrics in perfect Hindi, and the proper rhythm for the particular melody. Then Dilip would reconstruct the music for the songs.

Indira's experiences of contacting the Princess Mira were described to me as occurring in a state of *samadhi.*[2] Other schools of thought might describe them as either a psychic phenomenon or a manifestation of her own Higher Self, which she identified as Princess Mira. I asked for clarification of these differing viewpoints in order to have a better understanding of my own experiences. Dilip told me that he now accepts as fact that Indira, in the state of samadhi, directly contacts Princess Mira. He based his conviction on the frequency and consistency of the occurrences over a number of years, and on the fact that from the information Indira received, they were able to reconstruct the entire life of the princess.

When I arrived for satsang one evening I found that Dadaji was sick. He had been spending late nights on the roof of his house chanting, and had contracted a sore throat. People were told that for that

---

[1] Dilip wrote a play by the same name. Kumar Roy and Devi, *The Beggar Princess.*

[2] *Samadhi* is experienced in deep meditation; a return to Oneness.

reason there would be no satsang. They were reluctant to leave and Indira grew impatient with them. She questioned their sincerity and even accused some of considering their satsang a kind of entertainment, suggesting that if they had sufficient money they would spend their evening somewhere else.

Then she turned to speak to me, feeling that an explanation was in order. She spoke of the selfishness of people who, to gratify their emotions, would insist on having satsang despite Dadaji's illness. She also told me of the pain and anguish that she had undergone as a mother when she left her family and children behind to answer the call of the Divine.

At that very moment her little son, who might have been ten years old, interrupted us very excitedly and said to his mother, "Now that Dadaji is sick, why don't you call Mira and tell her to come and heal him?" Someday, not only this child who has had the privilege of being with her, but also all her children, will appreciate that in putting the Divine above everything, their mother showed herself to be extraordinary.

Dilip allowed me to record some of his songs, but unfortunately, I had neither the equipment nor the expertise to do justice to his voice, and so the recordings have never been reproduced in North America. I have used them myself though, to learn the chants and songs, and I am indebted to him for this service.

In the short time I was with Dilip Kumar Roy and Indira Devi, each of them taught me much—Dilip by helping me to understand the role of worship as a balance to the intellect in spiritual development, and Indira through her beautiful example of selfless devotion.

RESOURCES FOR THE READER

Suggested Reading

KUMAR ROY, DILIP, and INDIRA DEVI. *The Beggar Princess.* Allahabad: Kitab Mahal, 1955.

KUMAR ROY, DILIP and INDIRA DEVI. *The Flute Calls Still.* Bombay: Bharatiya Vidya Bhavan, 1982.

KUMAR ROY, DILIP and INDIRA DEVI. *Pilgrims of the Stars: Autobiography of Two Yogis.* Porthill: Timeless Books, 1985.

KUMAR ROY, DILIP. *Sudhanajali.* Poona: M. J. Shahani, 1958.

Indira Devi Center

Hari Krishna Mandir, Model Colony, Poona 411 016, Maharastra, India

Chapter 9

Anandamayi Ma

Anandamayi Ma means "Joy-Permeated Mother." She was first known to the West through the book *Autobiography of a Yogi,* by Paramahansa Yogananda. On my second visit to the Orient in 1958–59, she had been at Sivananda Ashram visiting Gurudev just a few days before my arrival, and some of the excitement of her visit was still in the air. Gurudev felt it was very important for me to meet another woman who was on the spiritual path. He emphasized that she, as the most spiritually powerful woman of India, would be an inspiration for me. As an example of his reverence and respect, he would join her for meals seated on the floor in the traditional way, as she preferred, instead of his custom of having his meals alone, sitting on a chair at a table.

By the time I arrived at the ashram, Anandamayi Ma had proceeded farther along the Ganges and was the guest of a maharani who was the member of parliament for the district. Gurudev arranged transportation

Swami Radha being called back by Anandamayi Ma to receive her special blessing and spiritual gift. "Sometimes just knowing of her support was enough to carry me though a difficult situation."

by taxi for me, along with a group of other people, so that we would be certain to meet her before she left again.

He told me that she had about twenty-five ashrams throughout India and that she visited each one once a year. It was her custom to stay no more than three days in any one place in order to avoid favoritism.

I knew that she had been married, and when her husband recognized her high state of consciousness he had made himself her servant. Although I was familiar with Yogananda's book and his reference to her, I did not know what to expect in a woman saint. But I decided just to take things as they came, which gave me an opportunity to practice surrender.

When we came to the summer palace of the maharani, we were taken to a garden house, what we would call a little guest cottage. This garden house was left entirely for Anandamayi Ma (whom everyone called "Mataji") as well as her mother, her travel companions, and some of her devotees. As we entered, they were chanting mantras and bhajans.

Anandamayi Ma, on the left with her ninety-year-old mother, a sanyasi.

There were mainly women and girls present, who all looked well dressed, as if they had come from good families.

Anandamayi Ma, wearing a white sari, was perched on a bed beside her mother who, at the age of ninety, wore the orange robe of a sanyasi, and had a shaven head. Mataji was about sixty, but she looked much younger. She had a lovely complexion, a beautiful smile, and striking black hair. She did not speak English, so the maharani and her son, as well as some of the visitors, served as translators. Just to be in her presence was a profound experience. Something radiated from her that was beyond words.

She did not give special attention to any of the visitors or followers who gathered around her. When our group left and I was walking slowly away, the maharani's son followed and asked me to come back because Mataji had something to convey to me. I was most surprised but very happy to return. She talked in Hindi to the maharani and her son, who translated the message.

First she asked me how much time I could set aside to think of her, and what time would be best once I was back in Canada. I figured

Anandamayi Ma and her mother meeting with a group that included Swami Radha and visitors from Canada, Africa, and Austria.

out that with the activity of the ashram, the time would have to be late at night, because I always had many people to see in the evening. By midnight I could really give attention to her. Then she said that at this time I should remember her, because she would give me an hour of her meditation at the same time in India.

I was amazed at her generous offer. She explained that she felt there was much to do in the West, that there were terrible times ahead, and she realized that I would need all the support I could possibly get for the work to be done. She wanted to help sustain me under all these influences because I was rather a new sanyasi (barely three years).

Her concern touched me deeply, since I, too, was worried about what lay ahead. The papers were filled with news of impending wars, of international clashes, economic collapse; there were revolts and riots in many places. I also considered that perhaps my own strength and development might be inadequate to meet the demands of a new ashram, that perhaps some of the difficulties lying ahead would come from

Swami Radha says of Anandamayi Ma, "Just to be in her presence was a profound experience."

within myself. The problems yet to come turned out to be both internal and external, and many times I have sent her a thought of deep gratitude for her help. Sometimes just knowing of her support was enough to carry me through a difficult situation.

I could understand the significance of making such a promise and sticking to it, but the depth of this obligation I fully comprehended only as time went by. To give a present of a book or flowers, or even to knit a sweater is one thing, but to give a spiritual gift of an hour of meditation every day for an extended period, is a tremendous commitment. No one who has not done this can appreciate what discipline is required. The mind can so easily get carried away with other things that it is difficult to keep that promise.

Sometime after my return to Canada one of her devotees visited our ashram and brought "The Song of the Mother." We would chant it often for Anandamayi Ma in gratitude for her thoughts and concern, which were truly expressions of divine love.

Resources for the Reader

Suggested Reading

Anandamayi Ma. *Words of Sri Anandamayi Ma.* 2d ed. Varanasi, India: Shree Shree Anandamayee Sangha, 1971.

Ray, Jyotish Chandra. *Mother Revealed to Me.* Varanasi, India: Shree Shree Anandamayee Sangha, 1972.

Yogananda, Paramahansa. *Autobiography of a Yogi.* Los Angeles: Self-Realization Fellowship, 1946.

Videotape

Sri Anandamayi Ma: Her Life and Her Message. Copyright: Matri Satsang.

Anandamayi Ma Centers

INDIA

Shree Shree Anandamayee Charitable Society, Bhadaini, Varanasi, U.P.
Publishing Division: 57/1, Ballygunge Circular Road, Calcutta 700 019

UNITED STATES

Matri Satsang, Box 1796, Nevada City, CA 95959

CHAPTER *10*

RAMAKRISHNA

While I was in Calcutta I visited the Ramakrishna Order, but I chose a bad time since it was officially closed to visitors. However, this may have been through some inner guidance rather than by accident, because the result was that I discovered another center of Ramakrishna's followers, called Ramakrishna Vedanta Math, where the resident swamis and the manager were extremely kind and helpful.

I was shown the various private rooms at the center, including the rooms of Swami Akhilananda and Swami Vivekananda. Again I had to adjust my ideas, this time about the path of renunciation and what it means to be a sanyasi. Here were rooms well-furnished with everything one might want, including beautiful antique beds that had been ordered from England, with hand-embroidered English linens and huge pillows.

I needed to clarify my thoughts: When is a swami a renunciate and when is he not? One swami in the group seemed to realize that I was puzzling over something important to me, and he encouraged me to ask questions. I was careful to ask in a way that was not offensive because I had no intention of insulting them, but I really wanted to know. The answer to the question of this apparent luxury was very simple.

The swami told me, "Our Swamiji lived his twelve years of tapas with nothing but his begging bowl and two sets of clothes, as tradition demands. But you see, the Lord is much more intelligent than people are. He does not let his pupil sit in the same class year after year. In twelve years you have learned a great deal about yourself through complete renunciation of physical comfort. After that, when things are given to you, you take them as a gift of God, who has now decided that you no longer have to sleep on a bare floor or on a tiger skin. So you don't reject what comes your way. Renunciation doesn't mean self-inflicted poverty."

As I pondered this, he felt that one more remark was necessary to be sure that I did not misunderstand him. "Of course, a sanyasi must not solicit gifts from anybody."

I was taken to the shrine of Ramakrishna and Sarada Devi, where oversized pictures of each of them were worshipped with oil lamps, flowers, and garlands. A vessel of water with a spoon beside it was also on the altar. I followed the swami, and put a little water into my hand, sipped it with a prayer that my spiritual thirst be quenched, and wiped my hand on the top of my head, to symbolically purify my thoughts. The water was sanctified by being in the shrine of Ramakrishna and Sarada Devi, a place where devotees chant, or meditate, or do *puja.*[1]

I was staying at a Buddhist center in Calcutta, and was most happy that the *bhikkhu*[2] who had accompanied me to the Math also showed great interest in this Hindu shrine. In fact, when the swamis suggested that I visit Belur Math and meditate in Ramakrishna's own room, the bhikkhu very excitedly offered to take me there as well. I noticed with delight the ease between followers of the two religions, and it gave me a feeling of great happiness and peace. I expressed my gratitude, and accepted his invitation.

Ramakrishna in his lifetime had seventeen disciples. Brahmananda, because of his extraordinary grasp of the teachings, was considered his spiritual son, a distinction given him unanimously by his brother disciples. Purushottamananda, who was so important in my own

---

[1] Puja is worship of the Divine through ritual, song, prayer, and meditation.

[2] A bhikkhu is a Buddist monk or mendicant.

Ramakrishna's room at the Belur Math, where Swami Radha's wish for quiet meditation resulted in an unusual communication with him.

development, was a disciple of Brahmananda; so I felt a personal link to these spiritual teachers.

My interest in the Ramakrishna Order was sparked not only by Ramakrishna himself, who was a great prophet at the turn of the last century, but also by Sarada Devi, a poor little village girl who became his wife. Reading about her life had been very important to me because there have been so few examples of women on the spiritual path.

When Sarada Devi arrived at Belur Math to take her position as Ramakrishna's wife, she was too young to understand the implications of living with this strange husband of hers. He was not just a temple priest, but a God-intoxicated man with an increasing desire to live the life of a brahmacharya. However, the temptation of enjoying sexual pleasures with his beautiful young wife created severe trials for him. With this young woman lying next to him on his small cot, he would carry on a conversation with himself, as if his mind were separated from the body: "What do you want? Here she is beside you. She is yours, your legal wife. Do you want to have the pleasure of this body? Or do you want to have the Most High? You cannot have both. You must decide."

The struggle to remain celibate in the dedication of their lives to the Most High was not an easy one for either of them. Ramakrishna found his most successful approach was to consider Sarada Devi as an incarnation of Divine Mother. For many years he had been a fervent worshipper of the Mother. So he prepared a very beautiful seat for her, surrounded her with silken cushions, and placed on her arms two golden bracelets studded with diamonds, which he had asked his devotees to obtain for him. He gathered flowers and made garlands, and then worshipped Sarada Devi as he worshipped Divine Mother. The young girl was bewildered at being a wife and yet not a wife, with this strange husband who seemed at times to be a madman. Later, when Ramakrishna was questioned, he claimed that it was Sarada Devi's extraordinary purity that made it possible for him to meet the test.

While Ramakrishna warned his disciples that women can be so attractive that they can be a diversion from spiritual life, he made a clear distinction between the worldly woman and the one with spiritual potential. His songs composed to Divine Mother are very moving and have a loving sweetness that is inspiring. His devotion to her can be compared to a worldly person who intensely pursues the peak of success in business, or devotes years to establishing an excellent academic reputation. The difference was that Ramakrishna's dedication was unswerving and without self-interest, and his single-pointedness was directed to his search for the Divine.

Ramakrishna was ill for two years before he died in 1886 of cancer. His illness and death brought many questions to my mind. Is spiritual purity reflected in the health of the body? What was Ramakrishna's karma? Was he taking on a disciple's karma? Why would anyone have to take on the sickness of another person? Had the disciples of Ramakrishna projected their physical and emotional problems onto their guru? Or did he willingly pick them up and take them into his own body? There were many unanswered questions at this time.

After Ramakrishna's passing, Sarada Devi experienced the loneliness and isolation of widowhood for ten years. Then she had visions of Ramakrishna telling her that she must gather the disciples together again. To do this, she went to the roof of their house, just as he had done, opened her heart to the Divine and asked, "Where have all my children gone? Send them back home to me."

In time, all the original disciples returned one by one, and many new disciples also came. They gathered around the Holy Mother, as

Swami Radha standing with Ramakrishna devotees outside the Math. "I was questioned thoroughly about why I had taken sanyas, how I had found my guru, Swami Sivananda, and how I understood being a sanyasi living in the West."

they called her, and she led them in carrying on the spiritual work, until her death in 1920.

These thoughts were in my mind as we arrived at Belur Math. I noticed that there were about twenty small cubicles in which people could meditate. Ramakrishna's room was packed with people, and the pillows on both beds were covered with flowers. I wanted some moments of quiet so that I could tune in to Ramakrishna, but thought it would be impossible with all the people there. I wondered, "Why are there so many people here now, when this is my only chance? I'm in

India for such a short time and they have many holidays when they could come."

Then in my mind I said, "Please let me meditate in peace." Within ten minutes the room was empty and nobody else entered. For a few minutes I sat in the corner trying to focus on Ramakrishna, and then I went to the *kamandalu*[3] and took some holy water to purify my thoughts.

As I tried to meditate and bring Ramakrishna into my mind I wondered about the very small temple, enclosed by a fence with an iron gate, where people who filed by had thrown more money before the picture of Sarada Devi than before the statue of Ramakrishna. Considering the position of women in India, I wondered at the simple village woman who was still collecting money for her followers thirty years after her death.

I had been concerned about my guru's command that I start an ashram. At this moment I could feel Ramakrishna's presence. Then into my mind came the thought, "Why do I have to have an ashram when there are so many people who are better?"

Suddenly I had an experience as if Ramakrishna were laughing his head off, slapping his knees, saying, "You are back in your Sylvia[4] aspect again. Why do you not stay as Radha? Then there are no questions."

I was irritated by his laughter, but after thinking about it I understood that my request for quiet was made through the Radha aspect, and the foolish worry came from Sylvia. As long as I remembered that, I would be all right. With the insight came a thrill as I realized that I had actually communicated with this saint.

Although I wondered at his laughter, which did not seem to be in keeping with the way a sage or prophet should behave, it did not occur to me in this ecstatic mood that Ramakrishna could not speak English. It was only later that I wondered how I could have received those impressions.

For years I kept silent about this experience, because I had no explanation for it. I accepted it within myself but I also questioned how it was produced. I felt that my mind could not possibly have created this event and the resulting sense of ecstasy, which lasted for days and gave me additional strength and energy. Again, I had more questions than answers.

---

[3] A kamandalu is a water container used by yogis during their spiritual practices.

[4] Before her initiation into sanyas, Swami Radha was known as Sylvia Hellman.

The shrine at Belur Math: Ramakrishna's picture is in the center, Sarada Devi's to the right, and Swami Akhilananda's to the left.

The next day we went to the library, where I was presented with books in which the swami in charge inscribed a dedication for me. Because everyone was busy during the daytime, I was invited to return in the evening, when a gathering for satsang would be arranged for all members, neighbors, and friends. I was asked if I would give a talk and also be prepared to answer questions. I felt very honored by this invitation and happily agreed to do so.

When I returned in the evening I was questioned thoroughly about why I had taken sanyas, how I had found my guru, and how I understood being a sanyasi living in the West. I answered as well as I could, and told them about my first experience with meditation in Montreal when I had met Swami Sivananda who was in India. I recounted my struggle to accept that as a true experience and not some sort of hallucination. Then I explained how I contacted him and received an invitation from him to Sivananda Ashram, where I received my training.

I tried to describe the way I lived this life in the West—through my own practices, and through teaching what I had learned, arranging prayer and mantra sessions, chanting and meditation, and giving brief talks followed by questions that I answered as well as I could. I also mentioned that I urged people to keep a spiritual diary. All these methods had come from my guru and had served me well, so I was happy to pass them on to others. Following my usual policy, I answered what questions I could, and when I had no answer I said so.

From my visit to Belur Math I had received inspiration from Ramakrishna, and gained further insights about the life of Sarada Devi. Much that I found in the books that were given to me I have used. Whenever my glance falls on them I recall the lessons that I learned from that visit.

RESOURCES FOR THE READER

Suggested Reading

GAMBHIRANANDA, SWAMI. *Holy Mother: Shri Sarada Devi.* Mylapore: Sri Ramakrishna Math, 1969.

ISHERWOOD, CHRISTOPHER. *Ramakrishna and His Disciples.* Hollywood: Vedanta Press, 1965.

M. *The Gospel of Sri Ramakrishna.* Translated by Swami Nikhilananda. New York: Ramakrishna-Vedanta Center, 1977.

NIKHILANANDA, SWAMI. *Holy Mother.* New York: Ramakrishna-Vivekananda Center, 1962.

Ramakrishna & Sarada Devi Centers

INDIA

Sri Ramakrishna Math, P.O. Belur Math 711 202, Dist. Howrah, West Bengal
Sri Sarada Math, Dakshineswar, Calcutta 700 076

UNITED STATES

Ramakrishna-Vivekananda Center, 17 East 94th St., New York, NY 10028

CHAPTER 11

FOUNDER OF MIRA SCHOOL~ SADHU VASWANI

Friends in Bombay took me to Poona to meet Sadhu Vaswani, who was better known as "Dadaji." He is the founder of the Mira School, which has since been dedicated to him in recognition of the work he has done for the education of Indian women.

In the Mira School little girls are admitted from the age of three, and they learn to chant verses from various scriptures, mainly the Gita. Dadaji believed that even if the little ones did not know what they were saying, they would be benefit from the spirit of holiness in these sacred texts and be supported by the spirit of the previous generations who had recited them.

When Dadaji found that I played the sitar and the harmonium, he immediately requested that I teach the children to chant the mantras of Radha and Krishna, particularly the one of Radha's longing for Krishna. We had chanting sessions for students and teachers. I gave talks, and afterwards was asked the question over and over again, "What attracted you to Eastern philosophy and teachings?"

Sadhu Vaswani, founder and principal of the Mira School. "Not only was his life totally dedicated to selfless service, but he was also very humble."

In return I was told the story of Princess Mira, after whom the school was named. An ideal for Indian women because of her example of saintliness, she was a fine model on which to mold the characters of little girls. Dilip Kumar Roy, in his beautiful play *The Beggar Princess,* has recreated the story of how, despite the luxuries and duties of royal life, Mira spent many hours in worship of Lord Krishna, chanting his name, and devoting her life to him. Her devotion to the Lord led her finally to leave everything behind and become a wandering mendicant.

Sadhu Vaswani had been a refugee from Sind who escaped the bloodbath that every revolution brings with it, and had begun to teach a number of little girls in return for food and shelter. In this way he found his path, which was to help Indian girls get an education. An eager student was never refused, even if the parents could not pay. Eventually he created a school for 800 children, and so gave employment to women teachers who have always had a great struggle in India, despite the fact that a woman became prime minister.

Not only was his life totally dedicated to selfless service, but he was also very humble. The first time that I met him, with folded hands and bowed head he asked me very sweetly, "Please bless me, bless me, bless

Swami Radha at the Mira School. "We had chanting sessions for students and teachers. I gave talks, and afterward was asked the question over and over again, 'What attracted you to Eastern philosophy and teachings?'"

me." I was a bit embarrassed but thought that this request was because of my orange robes, which indicated that I was an initiate, a sanyasi.

Dadaji's humility was outstanding in its contrast to the attitude of many men. Indian tradition demands that the woman worship her husband and take him as a symbol of God. This has certainly created much humility in the women, but has almost poisoned the character of the men. Many are so arrogant they consider their wives of no value except as producers of sons.

Dadaji was an old man when I met him, and his health was not good. He had chest trouble and somebody had to follow him around with a spittoon. Those who took care of him, in particular his nephew who carried the load of administration, tried to coax him to take walks in the sun. When my time came to depart and I wanted to say good-by and give him my last *pranam,*[1] I was told that Dadaji had gone for a walk.

After looking around for him, I finally saw a crowd gathered under a large tree in the distance. I went over to see if, by any chance, Dadaji could

[1] Pranam is a salutation of respect and devotion.

Sadhu Vaswani, also lovingly called Dadaji. "It was not important to him that he was getting tired at the age of eighty-two; he felt he had to be a constant inspiration and guide."

be there. Indeed he was. He could not just go for a walk; he thought that he must work always. It was not important to him that he was getting tired at the age of eighty-two; he felt he had to be a constant inspiration and guide. And so there he was, squatting in the dirt, and talking to the crowd.

By the time Dadaji had finished talking I had learned another lesson: no matter where we are, it is our duty to remind people of the purpose of life. Those who do not want to hear will wander off by themselves. Later I realized that speech is worthwhile only if it brings people together in word and thought on a spiritual level. Idle social talk does no good to anybody.

When I came to recollect what I had learned from various people I had met and what had made a lasting impact on my life, I found myself especially impressed by Dadaji's humility, and his message that one can never ask too many blessings. Dadaji, who asked everybody's blessing, has been a blessing to everyone he has met.

RESOURCES FOR THE READER

Suggested Reading

VASWANI, T. L. *The Voice of the Voiceless Ones.* Poona, 1968.

Sadhu Vaswani's School

Mira High School, 10 Connaught Rd., Poona-2, India

CHAPTER *12*

MEHER BABA

When I was in Bombay on my way back to the Himalayas, I took the opportunity to look for good bronze statues of the various deities to take home to Canada for our prayer room. I intended to put them on our altar as a reminder to focus our minds on the Divine.

A few days earlier I had visited the Elephanta Caves where I had seen images of Siva and Parvati, and they still lingered in my mind. The expressions on the faces of this god and goddess and the tenderness shown between them touched my heart, and brought a sense of serenity that left me without thought or words.

On entering the caves I could see the carvers' first attempts that had been abandoned and then, only a few hundred yards away, the magnificent finished work. Huge rooms with exquisite pillars and statues had been cut and chiseled with incredible precision, care, and inspiration, out of the same piece of rock. The skill, aesthetic sensitivity, and surrender to the unyielding material created something of such magnitude and beauty that I could only stand in awe.

The divine inspiration that was a driving force in the creation of these caves may be gone. But there are still millions of devotees today who worship Siva and who find in the relationship of Siva and Parvati, a continuous example on which to model their lives.

Other images that had been particularly attractive to me were the statues of Radha and Krishna at Swarg Ashram at Gita Bhavan. They were lifelike, soapstone carvings, not more than three feet high, and dressed appropriately for the various ceremonies at different hours of the day. The curved line of Krishna's body means "I am lenient with you because of your human nature. But I will remind you over and over again that you must turn your gaze to me, if you want to overcome the misery of life." Radha's attentiveness indicates ever listening within and without for the divine music of Lord Krishna.

In the Bombay shops I was searching for images like these, something tangible that could symbolize such inspirational ideas, and help the mind quickly refocus on the Divine.

In one of the shops, a lovely Indian lady approached me and asked who I was and where I came from. Her name has faded from my memory, but in my mind I can still see her smiling face and soft eyes. I can also hear the sweetness of her voice and her graciousness, which she expressed by saying, "Oh, you are interested in our Indian culture? Yes, times change, but there is still much here. I would be happy to invite you to meet a living saint. He is at my house right now. Please be my guest and come, if you have the time."

I accepted her invitation happily, and as we walked along the streets to her home she told me that his name was Meher Baba, that he had many wonderful devotees, and that he could see into a person's heart. He had kept silence for thirty years, and communicated with the help of an alphabet board on which he wrote his messages. It sounded very strange to me. If a person wanted to communicate, why use a board rather than speech? But I withheld judgment, keeping myself open and receptive. I had already encountered other strange circumstances that were unheard of in my own culture, and I had learned to appreciate things that were different. This I realized depended very much on myself and on letting go of my own preconceived ideas.

We came to a three-storey house on a quiet street of Bombay. People were lined up as they would be for a movie theater, three abreast, a long, long line, waiting to see the saint. Because the lady was

Meher Baba. "I received his blessing as his eyes burned like two big suns, and his beautiful smile came from the heart. I could see nothing but this intensity; the human being, the man, faded and disappeared."

the mistress of the house, I could follow her up to the second floor. People were standing on the staircase, but she led me past them straight to Meher Baba. I felt a bit uncomfortable, passing all these people who were patiently awaiting their turn. She left me in the room, motioning me to sit on the floor.

For four hours I observed a stream of people paying their respects to Meher Baba. He was buried under garlands of flowers that had been lovingly made to express devotion for the Divine, of which Meher Baba was a symbol. Every now and then several of his disciples would take off a number of them and relieve him of their weight, which must have been quite a burden. I had no garland and I had no fruits, which it is customary to bring to a guru, but at least I could bring an open heart and an open mind. And what I witnessed was something I had never seen before.

Meher Baba, dressed in white, was sitting in a soft chair that was covered with a cloth. He had a strange face; certainly he was not a handsome man by European standards. The people bowed or kneeled to touch their foreheads to his feet. He would then seize them by their shoulders or arms, pulling them up to him and giving them a warm embrace.

I was very surprised because I knew that embracing another person is very difficult for Indian people, particularly for those of the Brahmin class, who usually do not touch. A man must never touch a woman other than his wife; a father must never touch his daughter, or even call her by her name, but spell it out, or call her "daughter." But Meher Baba was a Parsee who did not have to comply with this custom.

He would then hold the person at arm's length and look into his or her eyes with an expression of love that took me through a whole range of emotions. First there was surprise, then admiration, then a feeling of sharing in the happiness of the one he welcomed. After several hours that same warmth remained, that expression of love directly communicated, bringing tears to poor and wealthy, young and old alike. There were very beautiful women who had saris with real gold threads woven into them that must have cost a fortune, but there were also men and women whose clothes were tattered, with bugs running up and down the folds of their rags.

Meher Baba never changed in the outpouring of his love. Although his face lit up differently, an old toothless, tattered man would get just as much of this deep loving expression as a beautiful young woman. Whoever was before him received the same love.

Then came a moment when Meher Baba motioned me to come close. I also bowed in reverence to him. I could do no less after having witnessed such a miraculous manifestation of love that I can only regard as divine.

I was a stranger from across the ocean, a woman from a different culture. Meher Baba pulled me up, too, and looked very deeply into my eyes for a few seconds—or was it an eternity? I received his blessing as his eyes burned like two big suns, and his beautiful smile came from the heart. I could see nothing but this intensity; the human being, the man, faded and disappeared.

The lady of the house came in and Meher Baba called her over, wrote something on his board and she nodded in agreement, then invited me to her inner courtyard. There, sipping iced tea, were forty or fifty of Baba's most devoted disciples. The impact of the beautiful light of love that I had seen in Baba's eyes was so great that all these details were almost blotted out.

His followers were considerate and loving, and seemed to have no jealousy. Such a group of people I had not met before. Perhaps it was because of the ecstasy they had experienced. They were concerned about the devotees in America, and I was given messages for them. The lady said, "Baba wants you to have the addresses of all his friends and devotees in America. Tell them of your meeting." This surprised me greatly and I was very moved by his gesture of trust.

I thanked this kind lady and went back to the Indian family I was staying with in Bombay, bubbling over with this marvelous experience.

Since then I have read publications about Meher Baba, some written by him and transcribed from the alphabet board. Again I asked myself with my Western logic, "Why not speak when God has given you a voice? If you want to communicate, why use a spelling board?" But does such speculation really lead anywhere? Is it not just my personal viewpoint to which I think I am entitled? Perhaps there is something to be discovered in this method that I have not yet considered. By now I had learned to keep any judgment or criticism suspended. This was Meher Baba's unique way. Why should I want him to give his message to the world differently?

So he became acceptable to me in his uniqueness. He demonstrated a kind of love that was all-encompassing, all-embracing, which I had to admit that I could not offer. I would have found it extremely difficult to have a face, distorted from the scars of smallpox, touch mine; to feel that skin on my skin; to smell the body odor from clothes that are not clean; to worry about the bugs that might get into my sari. So, with this insight, how relevant would my assessment of his kind of communication be?

This was a fine lesson to accept such physical closeness from all who would spontaneously open their arms, and how helpful it was to have learned! Later when lecturing in America, on one occasion I had accepted an invitation to an all-black church. Because I am a small person, I was picked up bodily by the members and embraced by some tall and stately black men and women. My "Divine Committee," as I call my divine guidance, had prepared me in time to accept people as they are, and to place my feelings of beauty and aesthetics in perspective. And so this helped me to look with gratitude into the depths of another human soul, unhampered by the influences of appearance and clothing.

Often when I go through my photograph albums from India, I turn to the one that has Meher Baba's picture, and feel gratitude welling up within me. My time with him paved the way for the work that was to be done later, 10,000 miles across the ocean. I have no picture of the gracious lady who, out of the generosity of her heart, invited a stranger to share an experience that was precious to her. But she, too, lives on in my memory and maybe someday we will meet again.

RESOURCES FOR THE READER

Suggested Reading

BABA, MEHER. *God Speaks: The Theme of Creation and Its Purpose.* New York: Dodd Mead & Co., 1955.

BABA, MEHER. *The Silent Master.* Compiled by Irwin Luck. North Myrtle Beach: Meher Baba Archives, 1967.

BABA, MEHER. *Twenty Fragments by Avatar Meher Baba. Bombay:* Meher Baba Centre, 1958.

Meher Baba Center:

Meher Baba Archives, 704 - 41st Ave. South, Building 18, North Myrtle Beach, S.C. 29582

Chapter 13

The Shankaracharya of Kanchi

Strolling through the streets of Madras, I passed a shop that had an unusual display of flowers and beautiful hand-carved antiques. I decided to go in and look around. There were not many flowers but there were many carvings. The owner came over to help me and I told him that I had an ashram in North America. I was looking for something that could be a focal point for the satsangs in the prayer room, which takes the place of an Indian temple. He spent at least three hours telling me about the background of some of these pieces, and in the end helped me to select a very fine carving that told the story of Siva and Parvati.

Mr. Murti, the shopkeeper, asked me to visit again, since he enjoyed having someone from the West who took such a deep interest in the carvings. Most Westerners who came to his shop either were tourists who had little appreciation for the symbolic meaning of Indian art, or the miracle seekers who wanted to take back with them stories of psychic happenings but who had no real interest beyond the sensational.

After he had packed my purchase, he invited me to stay and talk to him. There were certainly not many customers in the shop, so I accepted his invitation because I felt it would not be an inconvenience. He asked me to sit with him at a large table on which there were many papers and books. While we were talking his wife came into the shop, quietly made preparations, and included me in the afternoon tea that seemed to be their usual custom.

He was studying Sanskrit, he told me, and was busy translating some texts. "I am a devotee of the shankaracharya of Kanchi," he explained, "and he prefers to speak in Sanskrit, particularly if anyone asks profound questions." I inquired if it would be possible for Mr. Murti to get answers for a few questions that I had. After a long silence, he offered to introduce me to the shankaracharya, who happened at this time to be in the province just outside Madras. That was almost more than I could hope for. Mr. Murti said he would make an appointment for me.

There are four shankaracharyas, and they are the spiritual potentates for each corner of India. Within his own domain, each exercises the same kind of authority as the pope does within the Catholic Church. The shankaracharya selects as his successor a young boy about ten years old, who shows an aptitude for Sanskrit and an easy grasp of philosophical ideas, as well as a deep desire for learning. The training, which is very intensive, takes many years, and it is only upon the death of the shankaracharya that the succession can occur.

At the time I was staying at the Mahabodhi Society and the bhikkhus who were living there were very friendly and generous, spending much of their time talking to me and taking me to different places. On one occasion the manager unrolled for my benefit twelve beautiful *tankas*[1] that had been given by the Dalai Lama to the Society in commemoration of the Buddha's birthday. Through my conversations with the bhikkhus and their explanations of the meaning of this form of art, I was given an appreciation of, and insight into, tankas as a means of spiritual practice and inspiration. So here in the city of Madras I gained an understanding of two different art forms and their value in spiritual life: Buddhist tankas from the bhikkhus and Hindu wooden carvings from Mr. Murti.

At the time specified to meet Mr. Murti, I took a tonga, one of those shaky horse-drawn carts comparable to the Chinese rickshaw. The

[1] A tanka is a Buddhist wall hanging used for prayer and meditation

Swami Radha approaching the shankaracharya of Kanchi with her questions about maya and karma.

horses often collapse because they are so weak and undernourished. Their owners are very poor and care for them only enough to keep them alive. Sometimes I have hesitated to take a tonga because the animal was in such poor condition; and yet if I did not, the owner would have even less money and therefore less food for the suffering animal. So my consideration for the animal might not be helpful at all.

If the events of life are preordained by karma, what would be the karma of the poor horse, near starvation and continually beaten? How long would it have to suffer? What could it possibly learn, a poor creature that could know nothing of philosophical ideas, and would this kind of suffering serve any purpose? Was not the animal not just existing by its instincts? If it could understand, would that lessen its suffering? Would it be more willing to suffer?

I decided that if I had a chance to talk to the shankaracharya, I would ask him these questions: Is the theory of reincarnation born of our need to survive? And how can the karmic repercussions of the suffering of these poor horses be justified or understood? Human beings seem to be cruel to all kinds of animals, so even if the horse had the freedom to choose not to take birth as a horse again, would it be any better?

Mr. Murti and I went to see the shankaracharya where he was staying, at the home of an Indian family who felt extremely honored and specially blessed to have this illustrious person as their guest. He was sitting in the entrance of the house, wrapped in his orange robes with a crown of green leaves on his head. A devotee had put a flower into the leaves, indicating that knowledge had come to full flower in him.

I had been told that by custom the shankaracharya can travel only on foot or by elephant. Since the elephant is traditionally used by royalty, this symbolically equates him to royalty. When he travels on foot, he becomes the equal of the holy men who travel on foot throughout India. If a shankaracharya were to use modern methods of travel, such as automobile or airplane, he would lose his high position. Therefore, by these restrictions, he is confined to his own land, even today.

However, when I saw the way he huddled on the mat, it was hard to picture him riding in spiritual majesty on an elephant. Various people were standing about, more women than men, everybody keeping a respectful distance. I could see that this tradition, while it was extremely valuable in ensuring respect for the shankaracharya, would restrain further enquiry. Tradition binds him as I had been bound by my traditions, and I realized that there was no freedom from this, even for one as spiritually advanced as he.

I was undecided which question I would put to him first. Now that I was aware of teachers' peculiarities, I knew that I could expect to get an answer to one question but not another, or to get no answer at all if the questions were uncomfortable to him.

At the ashram I had been instructed in the idea of *maya*[2]—that everything is only apparent, only illusion. Did this mean that karma, too, is only illusion? I was having difficulty fitting together the different ideas I had been given. My question to the shankaracharya, when my turn came, was: "I have been instructed in the six stages of samadhi leading to complete Liberation, but whatever the concepts are, belonging to whatever school of thought, and considering also the differences in the meaning of Liberation, does not all that belong to maya?"

---

[2] Maya is illusion.

It is not easy for a Westerner to read the face of an Easterner, but it seemed to me that he was partly surprised and partly angry or irritated. While earlier his speech had been in English, slow and well-modulated, with his voice controlled, now he became agitated, and spoke rapidly in Sanskrit. My companion, Mr. Murti, nodded his head, then asked a couple of questions and responded with a few words, all in Sanskrit. He glanced at me and indicated that if I had any other questions I should write them down. Then he motioned me to leave with him.

When we were again seated in the tonga, which had been waiting outside the compound, he explained to me why the shankaracharya had become agitated. I had asked a very profound question in the presence of simple people whose faith might have been shaken, who might misinterpret the question and its answer, from lack of understanding and an intelligent grasp of such ideas.

For that reason he had answered in Sanskrit and had said, "Tell Mataji never to do this again because she might interfere with the fundamental faith of a simple or uneducated person." He also pointed out that a person who is a pure *bhakti*[3] would feel lost if even the beautiful expressions of love and devotion were grouped together as illusion.

I understood, and regretted that my own eagerness to know had caused me to express myself in a way that was, at that moment, out of place. The shankaracharya had provided me with the answer, but also with the message that the answer was not to be passed on to those who are simple and uneducated in spiritual understanding, even in the West.

The philosophy of maya I have seen misused to avoid dealing with an unpleasant fact. I heard a young doctor who was dabbling in Eastern teachings, say to the friend of a patient whose leg was to be amputated, "You don't understand. It is all maya, it's just in his mind." Such oversimplification is more dangerous than simple ignorance. I wondered how the doctor would have reacted if the leg had been his own.

There are many levels of reality and each has its place, just as there are many levels of mind with different purposes. While we are in this body we have to deal with the reality of the physical world. The Western tendency to intellectualize, to classify and categorize without really understanding, can do more harm than good. It takes a great deal of maturity and the knowledge that comes from practical experience to really understand maya.

---

[3] Bhakti Yoga is the yoga of love; love without a "because" attached to it, without asking anything in return. Also a bhakti is a yogi whose path is devotion and love.

Chapter 14

The Ganges Cave Dweller~ Purushottamananda

Swami Purushottamananda lived in a cave near the holy river Ganges for almost forty years. I met him at Sivananda Ashram when he visited my guru, during my first trip to India. When I saw him I immediately gave him the name "Dear God in Heaven," because he resembled the picture I had in childhood of what God must look like. His snow-white hair, surrounding his head like a halo, contributed to his saintly image.

The contrast between him and my guru was very marked. Swami Sivananda was a towering six feet two inches, while Swami Purushottamananda was barely five feet two. Swamiji's physical frame was slight and appeared even smaller when he walked next to my guru. Their way of life was just as different as their appearance. Sivananda Ashram was brimming with activity, but Swamiji's place was hidden away and very quiet; he accepted no disciples.

To reach his cave one had to know the entrance to the small footpath off the main road, and even that was only a dirt road used by the hill tribes when they came down with their cattle in the winter. The cave was scarcely visible, its only opening being to the Ganges whose waterline was very close.

When I visited him, at my guru's urging, with a group from Sivananda Ashram he tried immediately to make me feel at ease by telling the story of the cave. In the eleventh century a great scholar by the name of Vasistha had occupied it and there had written numerous commentaries on scriptures. Today these command the same reverence as the scriptures themselves. The place was named Vasistha Guha in honor of him, *guha* meaning "cave" in Hindi. It was a formidable size, disappearing far back into the earth, with a rock face polished by the passage of time and water. It was thought to have been formed by an underground stream that poured into the holy Ganges and that had dried up at some time in the past. When Swami Purushottamananda discovered the cave some forty years ago, he found the droppings of mountain lions, indicating that it had served as their den. Thirty feet into the mountain he had closed off the rest of the cave with a low stone wall. A wooden platform served as his place for meditation. And there he lived in complete solitude. He told us how he struggled with his fears when he first occupied the cave, not knowing whether or not a lioness and her cubs might also be using it.

Before he was initiated into sanyas, Swami Purushottamananda had received a degree in engineering from a university in southern India, which was his homeland. In his mid-twenties he had come to the Himalayas in search of a guru, whom he had found in one of Ramakrishna's great disciples, Brahmananda.

When he first moved into his cave, he would have died of starvation had not some hill tribesmen discovered him and brought him milk, butter, grains, and whatever of their meager possessions they could share with him. In return for this generosity he taught their children to read and write, and to recite the scriptures.

While the summer heat can be intense, the Himalayan winters and winds are very cold. These temperature changes affect the body very strongly. One would not think that with his fragile body, he could spend the winters there, and it was no surprise when I found that his limping was caused by arthritis in his hip. He told me that at one time the pain had become so great that he had thrown himself into the Ganges, because like many Hindus, he believed that the holy water would relieve his suffering.

By now I had heard many stories about the holy Ganges and how it healed people or transformed them. I could not help but wonder

Purushottamananda with other swamis in front of his cave entrance. "He told us how he struggled with his fears when he first occupied the cave, not knowing whether or not a lioness and her cubs might also be using it."

why he had not been healed, especially since he lived right on the river and took his daily morning bath there. Before I could ask about this, he said, "Westerners have too much attachment to the body and its comforts." This was certainly true for me, but what about the healing power of the Ganges? Is there always some karma that has to be paid off, even after enlightenment? He told me that the body also signals when to get yourself in order because your time is up. His remarks left me with much food for thought.

At our first meeting, when one of the visitors wanted to take a picture of him, he motioned me to a seat in front of his meditation hut. Before anyone realized what was happening, he dropped himself into my lap. It was so unexpected that I had to tense my muscles to keep my balance and hold him steady, although he was very light. When asked what he was doing, he replied with great simplicity, "I am her little child. I am sitting in Divine Mother's lap." While pictures were being taken I thought about this. He could see the Divine in everybody, but I was still having difficulty recognizing my own divinity.

On several occasions he invited me to meditate in his cave. It took awhile to get used to the darkness, and I thought I might feel uneasy sitting there all by myself, surrounded by rock, but the quietness was very peaceful and helped me to still my mind. The first time I went I suddenly began to hear some beautiful sounds, like singing from little birds, very lovely and sweet—a most happy and surprising experience. I took the flashlight Swamiji had given me to find my way into the cave and let its light play over the polished rock walls. There were no nests, no young birds, not even any bats. The walls were so smooth that dust could find no place to settle. Deciding that meditation was not possible, I came out of the cave into the sunshine where Purushottamananda was, and he said, "Now she has a smile on her face. She must have had a nice experience."

I took this as an opportunity to express my surprise. "What was that lovely singing, like little birds?"

He laughed. "You don't understand anything yet. Didn't it ever occur to you that rocks could have a voice, too?

Singing rocks! I was very surprised. He continued, "Everything has a voice. The universe is made up of sound and vibration. Everything has a voice, but human beings just do not hear."

The time for departure had come. As I gave Swamiji my pranam, he asked me if I wanted to come for a retreat. He said that I could stay in a small cave near his. I hesitated to give him an answer because I felt that I must first ask Gurudev Sivananda. He respected my hesitation, and took the opportunity to speak to the group about loyalty and consideration to the guru.

There was no difficulty obtaining permission from Gurudev. Three days later, arrangements were made for another visit to Swamiji, and that gave me time to ponder his words.

I felt elated at the thought of staying in his cave. I even anticipated some extraordinary experience. Swamiji, in spite of his limping, led me to the cave. It was part of the same rock formation as his big cave. Originally it was just a hollow in the rocks and it was covered by a wall of stones cemented together. Of course there was no window, and the door consisted of metal bars about six inches apart, through which rats and snakes could easily go in and out, but which gave protection from any larger beast. Inside there was a cement slab for a bed, and a steel bar for hanging clothes.

In the evening Purushottamananda instructed me to get up early the next morning to meditate with him. It was easy to awaken early because the bed was at such an angle that the sun, rising over the

"Swami Sivananda was a towering six feet three inches, while Swami Purushottamananda was barely five feet two. Their way of life was just as different as their appearance."

Himalayas, shone directly onto my face. Awakening to this majestic scene, I had no difficulty envisioning the Himalayas as "the rooftop of the world." But my body felt stiff and bruised; a blanket on concrete was not enough to make sleep comfortable.

As I was stepping out of the cave, I encountered an enormous snake—about seventeen feet long and thicker than my arm. I became paralyzed with fear. I had never before seen a snake that large except in the zoo, behind a glass partition, and I had no way of knowing if it was poisonous or not. For two hours we faced each other. I tried desperately to stay as motionless as the snake. Finally it disappeared, but it went down the same path I had to take to reach Purushottamananda! My heart felt as if it would jump out of my throat. It took all my courage to move on.

When I arrived at his hut after what seemed an eternity, he was surprised, but had a smile on his face. I told him about my encounter with the snake and, with gales of laughter, he said, "That was the python. You invaded its territory." With that, he offered me hot milk to calm me and give me a chance to regain my composure. Before he had a chance to remind me, I took the words out of his mouth and said, "No, I cannot yet see God in a snake that, for all I know, might be unfriendly to me."

On my return visit to India I saw that during the three years I had been absent, changes had been made that I considered good and practical for Purushottamananda. People had collected money, and, with the help of the mountain tribes, a small home had been built for him. It had three rooms downstairs in which others could stay, and an upper room with a bit of a roof garden for Swamiji himself. He lived there until his death.

When I visited him in his new home, he was sitting in his usual position, cross-legged on a cushion on the ground. This time there were more people around than there had been before, and I asked him if he had changed his mind and had taken on some disciples. He said that he allowed people to stay with him for a year, after which they must leave.

Purushottamananda was very particular about cleanliness and tidiness. The area in front of the cave was kept well-swept. Every time a leaf fell from a tree, he pointed it out to one of his students who had to pick it up and carry it away. This was his practical way of teaching people awareness. When I had first become aware that his visitors had to pick up the dry leaves and sweep the area around his cave several times a day, I thought he was being like a fussy housewife. But he explained to me that without cleanliness and tidiness in one's immediate surroundings, one cannot dare to invite the Lord.

He illustrated this beautifully by telling me the story of Lord Krishna and a devotee. "The devotee had observed all the rules and regulations, and had advanced sufficiently to submerge his mind in divine thoughts, using the image of Lord Krishna as a focal point. Finally the devotee complained to the Lord, 'Daily I spend many hours coming to you. Have mercy on me and at least come once to me.' The Lord granted the devotee his sincere wish and gave him a particular time when he would come.

Swami Radha with Swami Purushottamananda. "I felt honored and very happy to be with him once more."

"The devotee did a thorough housecleaning by opening the doors and the windows, and throwing everything out. When he had everything shiny and clean, he awaited the coming of the Lord. But when the appointed time had passed without the Lord's appearance, the devotee wept all night in sorrow. How could Lord Krishna break his promise?

"Then suddenly he became aware of the presence of the Lord, who said to him, 'I could not enter your house for all the garbage piled up outside.'"

Then Swamiji explained that the doors and windows are symbolic for the organs of sense perception and while the body and the mind need to be purified within, life in the world outside cannot be littered with the garbage of our selfish actions.

While he talked, he took my arm and led me to the little straw hut for meditation. I felt honored and very happy to be with him once more. The whole setting lent itself to peace and quiet, and although I felt peaceful, this meditation was not an exceptional one. Afterward one of his students served tea. Suddenly he addressed me, his face very serious, "You will come to the room on the roof. I will give you some special instructions." Visitors were moving around below, but they kept a respectful distance, knowing that when Swamiji was talking to a person, he should not be disturbed. He took his seat under the extended roof, protected from the sun. It had become his favorite place. As usual I squatted on the floor at a respectful distance.

At the start, our conversation was general. He remarked that it was only three years since he had last seen me and asked why my hair had turned white. I told him that I was probably worried about doing the right thing, running the ashram the right way, and so on. He started to laugh and made it clear I carried a burden that was not mine. At that moment I realized I had become duty-bound, even though I had understood intellectually that this was not the right attitude.

After a few moments of silence Swamiji talked a bit about himself; he said that he would give me the story of his life because I would need to know who he truly was. He would send the manuscript to me because I might not have the chance to pick it up. I assured him that I would: I could come by bus, and knew the paths leading through the jungle to his hermitage. Waving his hands, he said, "Yes, yes, I understand, but you will not come again." It was then that I knew he was talking about coming to India again during his lifetime.

He put a number of philosophical questions to me and seemed to be satisfied with my answers. On my first visit he had told me to purify my mind. He had also said that I must watch the scheming of my own desires to the exclusion of others, because only an impure mind does that. So it was with great relief that I now heard him say, "You have purified your mind; now I will give you a gift. You have a good understanding here," pointing to my head, "but now you must let it come down here," indicating the region of the chest. I had told him about the instruction in kundalini I had received from the Tibetan. He nodded his head as if he was very well informed.

Purushottamananda with Swami Radha and others in front of the new home that had been built for him. "You have purified your mind; now I will give you a gift."

"I see the mark of Lord Siva on your forehead." I was puzzled. "Come closer to me." So I moved closer, still keeping a respectful distance. "No, no," he said, so I moved a little closer, but it was still not close enough. Finally I moved so close that I was almost touching his knees. He bent over and looked at me for a long time. "Your first three chakras are open." He reached out with his hand and made a circular motion in the region of my heart, moving his hand up to my throat and continuing these motions on my forehead.

Unprepared and perplexed, my mind went blank. How long our meditation lasted I do not know, but suddenly Swamiji, with a voice like a child, cried, "Now I have nothing. You have become very different. I have given you all my power. I am a poor man. I have wondered about you, but it was only today that I saw Lord Siva's sign on your forehead, and so I obeyed."

He decided that I must leave immediately and led me along the path to the highway. The bus would take me to the ashram. His last instructions were that I should be silent about this experience, go into my room, lock the door, and spend the next three days in meditation. He said, "And remember, nobody will see you. You will be invisible to anyone passing you."

For the moment I did not fully realize the preciousness of Swamiji's gift and the sacrifice he had made. "Go on now. I will keep the young man who came with you here, so you can be alone. Remember, you will be invisible."

While I was on the bus I could not think of anything at all. Nor could I understand how it was possible nobody would see me. The ashram was brimming with people; I lived in the heart of it and would be returning when lunch was being served. The bus ride took about three-quarters of an hour. As I went to my front door, people passed me by, even children who always asked me for candies. Nobody talked to me. I was amazed! I was still conscious of the functioning of my body, so what made them unable to see me? I opened the padlock on the front door and went to the back door, pulling back the latch. After closing the padlock on the front door, I had to walk around the whole building to enter the room by the back door. Two women passed me and their eyes seemed to stare right through me. Without a smile or look of recognition they walked by. While I was going to the back door of my room I met three young men going for their lunch. They also did not seem to see me. I knew all five to be people who were talkative and curious. It was very strange.

Inside I bolted the back door and settled for meditation. I did not eat or have even a sip of water; most bodily functions seemed to stop. My conscious mind was dimmed. The surge of Energy was so great that it seemed to overtake me entirely. The recollections are beyond words, but now I knew from experience the state beyond mind.

It was much, much later, as I pondered the event, that I considered the possibility that the Energy was so enormous that it had shielded me from other people, had dimmed their minds and in fact made them look like zombies to me, like people walking around in a dream. There was no one in the room with me who could have told me if I ever moved from my place of meditation, or got up to stretch. Physical existence in the way I had known, all was removed as if by a thousand years. In fact, however I have tried to explain this experience or even voice it to myself, it was like seeing only the back of a beautiful tapestry.

On what must have been the fourth day I seemed to emerge from this ocean of nothingness, and slowly recognized the world around me once more. I wanted to open the door for a breath of fresh air. Still nobody greeted me or came toward me; a few notes were stuck to the door with messages for me. I felt as if I was expanded and as if I was all of the world around me; all the world was contained within me, and I was contained within all the world. Slowly this feeling of expansion changed, and by a gradual process I seemed to shrink back to the human body and mind I had known. It was some time before I could even remember my name.

I needed time to digest my experience, and could not resist the desire to understand what had happened. From this experience I knew, as my Tibetan guru had told me, that there are levels of intelligence, and that the god and goddess in each chakra represent the respective aspects of the six levels of consciousness. What I had vaguely understood before, now became clear.

I had often hoped and prayed that I would meet my Tibetan guru again. Through his peculiar method of teaching, he had skillfully taken away all those concepts on which I had founded my mental and emotional security. The Tibetan had laid a good foundation that had prepared me for the actions of Purushottamananda. But now this bliss and joy and knowing of the heart were so fulfilling that nothing else seemed to have value. Nothing else mattered. Life itself seemed like a burden, and the uselessness of action felt painful.

Swami Sivananda, whom I have always considered my personal guru, gave me the first impetus and taste of spiritual life. He recognized my desire, my searching. He guided my steps and made it very clear to me that I must stay on. I had started a work way back in time and this spiritual work must be finished. It was difficult to resign myself to it.

There are different temptations that present themselves along the way: to become a great teacher, to have large numbers of followers, to be a scholar or a pundit who knows all the scriptures by heart, to be a great healer, and so on. But here was a temptation that is little known: to leave the body.

Resources for the Reader

Purushottamananda had no disciples and gave Swami Radha all his power, as he said. Swami Radha's writing is the only known record of him. He was a disciple of Brahmananda, who was Ramakrishna's spiritual son. Readers may therefore wish to learn more about this lineage, and can refer to the bibliography of Ramakrishna included in this volume.

CHAPTER 15

THE BUDDHIST ABBOT~ PHRA BIMALADHAMMA

When I arrived at Bangkok, Thailand, the ride from the airport led us past an area that was set aside for the biggest world convention of Buddhists ever held. The Buddhist society had made a large contribution and Thailand had erected a huge statue of the Buddha, carved in wood and covered with gold leaf. It was an imposing and beautiful sight, and preparations for the convention kept many people busy.

Upon arriving at the Wat Madadhatu temple, I was met by one of the disciples with whom I spent some time in conversation. He gave me instructions in a technique that I have since given the name "Straight Walk," because it was the beginning of the practice of going within myself, and looking straight at the goal to which I aspired without losing time in sightseeing.

Inside the temple itself, the long corridors were lined with larger-than-life-sized statues of the Buddha. When I was introduced to Phra Bimaladhamma, the abbot of the monastery, he called one of his

English-speaking disciples to act as translator, and took great pleasure in showing me around the temple and the education center. The plan of the temple was similar to that of a medieval Catholic monastery: covered walkways, shaped by many arches, led from buildings to inner courtyards that had a *stupa*[1] or sometimes a water fountain in the center.

I inquired about the symbolic meaning of the Buddha statues in the long hallways. With a smile on his face, the abbot suggested that I walk down the hall once again and then come back. I did just that, and when I returned he looked at me questioningly, then asked me through the interpreter if I had found the answer.

I was a bit unsure. The statues had been cast over and over from the same mold, and they were very large. I said, "Each Buddha is the same. Does that mean that the Buddha is always the same?"

That answer was not quite correct, but I had come close.

"The Buddha is always the same with each step that you take, and each step that you have taken in walking down this hall, is it not telling you that you are continuously in the presence of the Buddha?"

It was so simple that I was surprised it had not occurred to me. I could have grasped the symbolic significance if I had made a greater attempt to understand when I had talked to the disciple outside. However, I relaxed when it became obvious that I was not expected to have the correct answer for everything. After all, I had come to learn.

The abbot also took me to a new building, urging me to follow him up the scaffold. He was very proud of this building, which would become his English department in the expanded education center. A shy young boy of eleven or twelve, dressed in a monk's robe and with shaven head, accompanied us and also clambered around the scaffolding. He gave me a sudden jolt by stepping back too far. I could see that with just one small step, he would have fallen to the concrete below. Quickly I grabbed him and pulled him away from his precarious position.

The abbot and interpreter were both horrified, and the little boy started to cry. The interpreter explained to me that my touch, because I was a woman, had defiled the young boy who had come for three months to live the life of a monk.

---

[1] A stupa is a sacred mound or monument housing Buddhist relics.

The Buddha statues in the long hallways at Wat Mahadhatu. "The Buddha is always the same with each step that you take, and each step that you have taken in walking down this hall, is it not telling you that you are continuously in the presence of the Buddha?"

I could not understand this reaction; it did not seem logical. I wondered if they would rather have seen the little boy fall off the scaffold and be badly hurt or even killed on the concrete floor. I had touched the child for an obvious purpose, and as a sanyasi wearing the orange robes, I was not to be considered a woman in the usual sense, even according to the ancient texts and traditions. Somehow I felt insulted, but I also remembered that women in the Orient have a very poor position. I had noticed a few women around the monastery and I wondered why they had come and how they were treated. The abbot cut the conversation short but graciously consented to an audience the next day, which surprised me after my obvious misbehavior in his eyes.

The next day we walked around the grounds and came to another building much more complete in its construction, and I was told that this was another expansion of a school to prepare students for higher learning. All this was very impressive and the abbot was most proud of the work. He kept encouraging me to compliment him on how modern, well-educated, and advanced he was. He also told me about his visit to Germany, and could not understand why I had gone to Canada and what I wanted in Thailand, when there were so many interesting places in Germany. He had talked to Catholic priests, bishops, archbishops, and had even had a visit with the pope. He had brought back several pieces of equipment and a big black umbrella, of which he was very proud. This amused me, but I was careful to keep the abbot—the administrator of an elaborate monastery and education complex—separate from the monk that he basically was.

There was no problem for me in taking pictures. The abbot carefully arranged his robes and told me, through another English-speaking monk, that it was not because of vanity. He was aware that, to anyone who saw my pictures, he would represent something more than himself as an individual, and that he had a duty to give the best possible impression. As a practical person, I found this understandable and acceptable. I was happy to have been given this explanation because of my temptation to think that men, particularly Oriental men, are vain.

Sometimes the abbot answered even before his monk had finished translating, and this made me suspicious that he did speak sufficient English to talk to me directly. But perhaps he thought his English was not good enough, so he preferred not to use it in front of a foreign visitor. I had an audience with him almost every day, lasting from two to five hours. This was very strenuous for my physical body because I

Phra Bimaladhamma who prepared himself carefully for this photograph. "He was aware that to anyone who saw my pictures, he would represent something more than himself as an individual, and that he had a duty to give the best possible impression."

had to sit still in a peculiar strained position that put great pressure on my knees, but it was most exciting and stimulating for my mind.

We talked about the mind and about psychic phenomena, which had greater importance for him than they did for me. He asked one of the monks to come and demonstrate some feats of psychic energy. He showed me another who he said could remain for many hours in deep meditation, but who appeared to me to be rather in a state of trance. It was important for me to learn that deep meditation and trance are two different things, and I was grateful to him for the opportunity to have these insights. I was careful not to disagree too often or question him too intently, because this might have led to misunderstandings and would also have appeared ungrateful. This is very important in the East.

Phra Bimaladhamma. "I was invited to participate in some of the temple activities, and it was a very elevating experience to hear the voices of 500 monks chanting the sutras.

Even the most sincere desire to know can be misinterpreted when the questions become too probing.

I asked him about the position of women in his country. His reply was that if one is first a good wife and mother, the rest will take care of itself, but there definitely must be no sexual relationship outside of marriage.

A Buddhist monk, even one who holds that position for only three months, must not even touch a woman or he is considered defiled and must start his three months over again. This prohibition seems to be meant not so much as a condemnation of women, but as a help for the monks to gain control over their sexual instincts and drives. Later I learned that sexual interaction with one's own sex was not considered immoral. It seemed that it was only regarded as sex when there was the possibility of offspring.

During my stay I was invited to participate in some of the temple activities, and it was a very elevating experience to hear the voices of 500 monks chanting the sutras. On my last visit with him, Phra Bimaladhamma was particularly charming, and told me that he had a present for me. He gave me a little box, and I tried unobtrusively to ask one of his disciples if I was expected to open it in his presence, or if I should take it to my room and look at it there. I was not familiar with the customs of Thailand and I did not want to violate the etiquette. But the abbot again must have understood my question, and he motioned me eagerly to open the box. He was very curious to see my reaction.

Inside was a very beautiful, tiny golden Buddha, a replica of one in the temple. He also handed me one of his writings on the complete *vipassana*[2] technique, which had been translated into English for Buddhists in the English-speaking world. I am most grateful to him, because many of these practices are not written down and it is very difficult to remember the details. The material provides excellent guidance in the practice of concentration and awareness, and in understanding their subtle effects.

From my time at the Thai temple, I was reminded how important it is to distinguish cultural traditions from the essence of spiritual practices. I learned a great deal both from my personal conversations with Phra Bimaladhamma and from his writing. The opportunity for me to meet a man of his education and stature was unique.

RESOURCES FOR THE READER

Suggested Reading

BIMALDAHAMMA, PHRA. *The Path to Nibbana.* Bangkok: Mahadhatu Monastery.

Monastery

Mahadhatu Monastery, Bangkok, Thailand.

---

[2] *Vipassana* is a Buddhist system of meditation based on observing the mind.

Chapter 16

The Catholic Stigmatist~ Padre Pio

On returning from India in the early spring of 1959, I stopped in Rome, drawn by fond memories of travels in Italy with my father, and a desire to somehow integrate my Western religious heritage with the Eastern spiritual one. What better place to do it than here in the very center of the Christian world, a place sacred to more than 500 million Catholics?

After visiting the Vatican and seeing many beautiful churches with their incredibly expressive paintings and statues, I decided to contact the woman disciple of Swami Sivananda, whose name I had been given at the ashram. She invited me to her house for dinner and though obviously very wealthy, she also showed herself to be quite an exception to her class. At the dinner table she invited her cook and maid to join us, asking me to kindly excuse this gesture. I felt very comfortable with it but wondered what had made her side-step, especially in the presence of visitors, the strict rules of etiquette. I made no inquiry, but from our later conversations I could guess what had influenced her.

She had visited a monk by the name of Padre Pio, who, she said, had all five stigmata. She told me his story and asked, "How long will you be in Rome? I think you should go and see him."

I immediately felt a very positive response, but then remembered, "I can't speak Italian. Would you come along?"

She said, "Oh, he comes from Naples and I don't understand his dialect either. But don't worry. He will understand you, even if you don't say anything."

So we talked for most of the evening about Padre Pio, and about Swami Sivananda in India, with whom she had been in correspondence for many years. She helped me plan my travels to Padre Pio's church: I could take a train to Foggia and then a bus to San Giovanni Rotondo. The monastery and the newly built hospital were just a mile or two up the hill.

The next day I got my ticket and boarded the train. When I showed the conductor my ticket, he held my hand and smiled and gestured for me to follow him. As I couldn't speak Italian, I didn't know if there was something wrong. But at his compartment, his intentions became very obvious when he tried to put his hand inside my blouse. I fought him off as gently as I could by saying, "I'm going to Padre Pio. I'm going to Padre Pio." That set him back a bit. Finally after I repeated the name a few more times, he looked at my ticket and let go of me. I felt that already, without having met him, I had experienced the padre's protection. Nevertheless I was disturbed that women the world over remain victims to those men whose minds are filled with nothing but their own sexual gratification.

By the time the bus arrived at San Giovanni Rotondo I had calmed down. I walked around on the plaza and discovered a nice-looking small hotel that was very pleasant, very clean, with all the modern comforts, including hot running water and a telephone in my room. The host and hostess, who spoke several languages, advised, "If you want to meet Padre Pio, five o'clock is the first mass in the morning, but you have to be there at least an hour before then. Hundreds of people try to get into the little church."

Why did I want to go? I realized that the woman in Rome was a disciple of Sivananda yet also had a connection with Padre Pio. She moved between two worlds, East and West. I, too, was born and brought up in the West and yet had been called to India, in a quite unusual way. I also had a burning question to ask Padre Pio: Do I have a spiritual mission? Since I was very young I had been told about this "mission" but had rejected the idea. "Mission" reminded me of missionaries, and I certainly had no desire to be a missionary, either Eastern or Western.

Reading a book on Padre Pio I had picked up that afternoon, I found that apparently he was not interested in answering questions or having conversations, and that he listened only to confession. I wondered how meeting with him could settle my concerns; nevertheless, I went to bed very early, preparing for the possibility.

I was at the chapel by 4 A.M. The crowds were already enormous and I was appalled by their behavior—they pushed, pulled, and elbowed their way in. One little nun held a footstool against her chest with the legs sticking out, to force her way into the chapel. People in different cultures have different temperaments, I realized, and perhaps here one had to be hot-headed to get anywhere. But this way of being was so contrary to the quietness of meditation I had experienced in the Himalayan ashram. I did not fight my way into the church, but just turned around, hoping there would be fewer buses with fewer people the next day. But the next day it was exactly the same. Again I decided not to battle my way into the church, and instead, like many other people, I took a leisurely stroll in the surroundings.

Many eyes focused on me because I was wearing my orange sari,[1] something they had probably never seen. It was later in the afternoon when a young woman approached me. She said she could not help herself, but she wanted to touch the silk.

She asked. "Is it comfortable?"

"Oh yes, very comfortable. It's a woman's dress in India, but the color, orange, shows something different; it's similar to being a nun in the West."

We talked a little more and she asked me, "Have you seen Padre Pio?"

"No."

"You have not gone?"

"Yes, but I would not enter the chapel, struggling and behaving in such a way. So I think I will probably leave tomorrow."

"No," she said, "you must meet Padre Pio. But if you are a kind of a nun from another tradition, why did you come here?"

So I gave her some of my background—how I had met Swami Sivananda in meditation and had been called to India—and told her my

---

[1] An orange sari is worn by women initiated into sanyas. I was one of the first women of the West to take these vows.

desire to hear from a Western teacher that different religions were only different expressions of the one Truth.

Then she wanted to know where I came from. "Are you Indian?"

"No. Canadian."

"But you speak German."

"Yes. I immigrated to Canada from Germany some years ago."

It seemed she was very curious and wanted to talk more. As I was getting tired, I invited her to the hotel for coffee or tea. But when she checked her watch, she said she would have to excuse herself to keep her time of meditation, and she left.

I read a little more from the book on Padre Pio. He apparently could read people's minds; he was said to be able to bi-locate or be in two places at once, with his presence detectable by the distinct smell of roses and violets; and he was said to have an incredible ability to look into the human soul.

At five o'clock the next morning, my phone rang. I let it ring. Who would phone me? I didn't know anyone here. Nobody knew me. But because the phone kept ringing, I finally picked up the receiver. A voice asked, "Is this the lady in the orange robe? Padre Pio will see you at eight o'clock this morning. I will come and get you."

I recognized my new friend's voice and asked her if she could come earlier so we could have breakfast together. She agreed happily. It never occurred to me to ask her how she had arranged the appointment so quickly. Over breakfast I learned that she was a schoolteacher and had come here often to meet with Padre Pio. As we prepared to leave for the church, she said, "I know the monks and I'm sure I can get you in to see him."

The crowd was as fiercely determined as before and would not let us through. But my friend found a monk she knew and told him about my appointment. He helped us to the front of the church, then asked the people to offer me a chair. They wouldn't. They were looking at me with very hostile and jealous expressions. I was a foreigner and an intruder.

I did without the chair, and sat cross-legged in Indian fashion on the beautiful mosaic floor. Immediately I realized I must be sitting in front of Padre Pio's confessional, because I saw a window covered with a curtain.

How would I go about confessing? I couldn't think of anything so fast. Even if I could remember things from recent years, at this moment I certainly could not recall serious misdeeds that I must have committed years earlier.

"He apparently could read people's minds; he was said to be able to bi-locate or be in two places at once, with his presence detectable by the distinct smell of roses and violets; and he was said to have an incredible ability to look into the human soul."

Before I could finish my thoughts, the curtain was drawn aside and there was Padre Pio looking at me with piercing eyes.

I quickly decided on a purely mental conversation. I said in my mind to him, "I don't speak your language. I have never been to a confession and I would not be able to remember all my faults. I can do one thing: I will give you access to the back of my mind so you may see everything there is."

After a pause, again just in my mind, I asked him, "Is it true that I have a spiritual mission, as I have been hearing for nearly all of my life? If this is so, please show me a sign by raising your right hand."

At the moment I put this question to him, I was inwardly very calm and prepared for a negative answer more than for a positive one, because I was not convinced that I had the qualifications to have a mission in my life.

But the padre reached out his arm. His right hand rose very slowly. All the while, he was looking at me. I was astounded and I suddenly felt my heart beating fast. I was so much in the grip of the event that I did not quite know how to formulate my next question, which was of equal importance to me: "Is it true that all religions are valid, though perhaps different expressions of mankind's understanding of the spiritual quest? Does God have many names, many forms? If this is so, please stretch out your left hand."

I kept my eyes focused on him very intently. Slowly his left hand reached forward.

Then a thought spontaneously arose in my mind. I mentally asked him, "This being so, then you would not object to blessing this rosary and also my Indian mala, which I use to chant mantras?" With a touch of anxiety I silently asked, "Will you bless them?"

I had stretched my hand out toward him, holding the rosary and the Indian mala. His hand fell in benediction over my hand. I then put both sets of beads quickly around my neck.

I realized that there were lots of people waiting for their confessions. Padre Pio had most graciously given me what I needed to remove the greatest worries and heaviness from my heart.

I rose and while standing before him, raised my hands over my head, hands touching. It was the traditional Indian greeting, *"Namaskar"* (Glory to God). To my astonishment, he returned the same salutation, and then drew the curtain back.

My most precious audience with Padre Pio was over.

As I left the church, people in the crowd stepped back and made room for me. In their faces, the hostility and the jealousy were gone. It seemed that something had touched them also.

As I reached the door I met the young lady who had arranged this incredible event for me. She was overjoyed and wanted me to tell her all about my meeting. I declined, saying, "I must spend some time

"Padre Pio had most graciously given me what I needed to remove the greatest worries and heaviness from my heart."

alone. I hope you understand. I'm very, very deeply moved. I wouldn't find the words right now. But it's still early in the morning, why don't we meet later at the hotel?" She agreed. She understood.

During lunch I asked her how she had made the appointment. She smiled. "Padre Pio is my spiritual father. I told him in my meditation that you had come from far away, and that I couldn't bear for you to leave without having met him. He said to bring you at 8:00 A.M."

I was stunned. I then told her how Padre Pio had answered all my silent questions by his gestures.

The entire episode surrounding Padre Pio made such a deep impression that it stayed with me for years to come. But the mind being what it is, I sometimes wondered and doubted, Was Padre Pio just being kind? Did he really think I was just one of those lost heathen souls that he needed to save? Would he, if he could, visit me at the ashram here in Canada?

As if to still my doubts, that experience also came.

The first time Padre Pio made his presence undeniably known was during an evening when I had arranged to have a lecturer speak at our

Vancouver bookshop. One of my students was helping me set up chairs and organize the room. Having had a busy day, we went to eat dinner at a tiny restaurant just two doors from our place. We put a note on our door describing where we were, so that if our guest lecturer came early he could join us. After a few moments he did show up, and the two men began to talk (as is usually the case), and I was left to my own devices.

For some unknown reason Padre Pio came to my mind.

Suddenly the visitor said, "You are using a beautiful perfume. May I ask what it is?"

I simply said, "No, it's not available anywhere. It's not really my perfume."

He said, "I don't understand."

I responded, "It's not the place to talk about it but I'll tell you later." However, because the event was not important to him, he never came back to the subject.

The restaurant was as long and narrow as a hallway, with chairs and tables only on one side. The ventilation was extremely poor. It was amazing to me that here—where the smell of cooking was so intense that most people simply ate quickly and left—the perfume of Padre Pio was still stronger, so strong that a stranger could become aware of it.

I left the remaining arrangements of the evening's lecture to my assistant. I had to ponder over why Padre Pio had come. What was I specifically supposed to do tonight? The answer could come only in meditation.

Another time at Yasodhara Ashram on Kootenay Lake, I had an equally strong confirmation of Padre Pio's presence.

A couple who had been Catholics but had lost faith, tried to look for answers elsewhere. Some of my students had told them that they could talk freely to me, because I would not try to convert them into something that they were not, but I would be open enough that they could discuss their doubts.

Because they were Catholics (though somewhat absent from or perhaps just absent-minded about their original religion), from the moment that I met them and listened to them, I began invoking Padre Pio in my mind.

At one point in the conversation the husband suddenly said to me, "A woman like you should not wear any perfume."

I said, "But I don't wear perfume. I don't even have any. What is it that you smell?"

The husband looked at his wife, "Do you smell this, too?" She nodded her head. He said, "What would you say? Is it roses? Is it violets?"

And she said, "It could be both."

I smiled. Good. So once again Padre Pio had made his presence known, from thousands of miles away and across an ocean to here in the Rocky Mountains of British Columbia.

I had often mulled over in my mind, If Padre Pio did understand that God can have different names, different shapes and forms because of the different cultural perceptions, then why did he never write about it? Why did he never say anything to someone who could publish it? Many books had been written about his work and I had read as many as I could, looking for just that point. Why had he never written, "God is everywhere. Different religions only give different names and forms, depending on people's ability to perceive the Divine." This question kept lingering in my mind.

One night I had a dream. In the dream Padre Pio said, "Because I am an obedient son of the Church, I must not do or say anything that would be contrary to what the Church teaches." At that moment in the dream I saw masses of people. I understood then that perhaps he could talk about this to individuals, but not to the masses. With his appearance in my dream, Padre Pio had dispelled my last doubt. I felt my mind at peace, and grateful for his compassionate answer to my every question.

One day in the fall of 1968, after a long absence of Padre Pio's perfume, I was suddenly filled with very powerful memories of him. That night a visitor came to some classes that had been arranged months earlier. She brought a little notice that Padre Pio had died the same morning, September 23, 1968.

RESOURCES FOR THE READER

Suggested Reading

CARTY, CHARLES MORTIMER. *Padre Pio: The Stigmatist.* St. Paul: Radio Replies Press, 1952.

THE DUCHESS OF ST. ALBANS. *Magic of a Mystic: Stories of Padre Pio.* Clarkson N. Potter, Inc., 1983.

PARENTE, PASCAL P. *A City on a Mountain: Padre Pio of Pietrelcina.* St. Meinard: Grail Publications, 1952.

Padre Pio Centers

ITALY

Santa Maria delle Grazie, San Giovanni Rotondo, 71013 (Foggia)

UNITED STATES

U.S.A. National Center For Padre Pio, 11 N. Whitehall Road, Norristown, Pennsylvania 19401

Chapter 17

The Dalai Lama

Buddhism has always been of special interest to me. Swami Sivananda knew this and often referred to my way of sticking my hands into my sleeves, which is a Buddhist custom to promote stillness of the body and mind. He would also occasionally remark, "She has a soft spot in her heart for Lord Buddha."

Although in my parents' house various Buddhas were on display, mainly Chinese ones, they were seen more as pieces of art than as reflections of spiritual ideas. The concept that the image of the Buddha is a reminder to pursue the state beyond mind, came to me much later when I stayed in the various monasteries referred to elsewhere in this book.

During earlier times, when it seemed the political situation would bring Germany and the rest of Europe to the brink of disaster, I felt tremendous fear and a certain anxiety that left me without focus or direction. In the most intense moments when fear really gripped my heart, an image of the Buddha seemed to come from nowhere, took on a life of its own, and floated in front of me even while I was moving about. Then the

Buddha grew to the size of a four-storey house. I had a natural response to move underneath his huge, protective form, and there I felt peaceful and secure. After the first experience, I intentionally placed myself in the lotus posture, and aligned my spine with the Buddha's. Then something extraordinary occurred, difficult to describe, except to say that I seemed to disappear into the body of the Buddha. Over all these years the impact of these experiences has stayed with me.

A year or two later, when my husband and I visited my father, I was given another clue about my attraction to Buddhism. The conversation centered around sons and daughters, specifically my husband's desire for our firstborn to be a son. My father said that he had been rather happy to have a daughter, and produced a diary of my early childhood days with details that astounded me and convinced me that I was indeed very special to him. He read one of the stories from the diary: On returning home one day he had found me in his study, sitting cross-legged in the middle of the room, with my eyes closed. Surprised at such an unusual position for a four-and-a-half-year-old, he asked what I was doing, to which I replied, "I play death, and when I do this I should not be disturbed." I showed him how I could hold my breath, and said that was what I meant by playing death.

There had been no other specific indications of my affinity for Buddhism until around the time I went to India. Before I went, I was given the book by Evans-Wentz, *Tibet's Great Yogi: Milarepa.* The word *Milarepa* held my attention, and into my memory came a dream. I had been regularly recording my dreams for several years, and it did not take long to find this one. In the dream a movie theater was going to show a film of Milarepa's life story, so I purchased a ticket and went in. Though there had been a long line-up outside the theater, I was the only one in the audience. Across the screen in large capital letters was spelled out, M-I-L-A-R-E-P-A. The dream had left me puzzled, because at the time I had no knowledge of this Tibetan yogi, who attained liberation in one lifetime. Then the book by Evans-Wentz fell into my hands and has been a source of inspiration and study for me ever since.

While in India I wanted to travel to Tibet, but the political situation was such that no permits were issued except if a traveller was accompanied by two officials. These restrictions were too demanding for my strained finances so I had to let my desire go. A few years later when the Chinese invaded Tibet, many in the Western world formed Tibetan Aid Societies. I was given the opportunity to help the one in Vancouver by collecting money and by finding foster parents for Tibetan orphans.

In this activity my affinity with Tibet and its teachings found a useful expression.

My long-cherished attraction to the Tibetan teachings was confirmed through my relationship with the Tibetan guru. But the culmination came when I met His Holiness, the fourteenth Dalai Lama in 1980, in Toronto, Canada. Some dear friends had arranged an interview with him to discuss ways to help the economic situation of Tibetan refugees, so they arranged for my meeting at the same time. His Holiness was also concerned about resettling several thousand Tibetans who were then hosted by Nepal. While the business conversation with the Dalai Lama was going on, I looked at the little color photograph I was holding. It was of the White Tara that I had embroidered. I had copied the outline from a poster onto a piece of fabric, then matching the threads with the original colors as closely as I could, I had embroidered, remembering her mantra with each stitch.

When His Holiness agreed that I could have a few words with him, I placed this picture in front of him. He was surprised and said, "Oh, what is this?" After a closer look, he continued, "Oh, it's Tara, the White Tara," and looking up to me said, "How is this?"

I explained that I had made this embroidery the size of a tanka. My motivation, because I am a woman, was to get in contact with a divine female aspect. The stories of spiritual struggles that have come down through history are all about men; there are few to serve as an example for the woman of today, like myself.

His Holiness picked up the picture and touched it to the top of his head, then put it on the pile of the business papers, and looked at me with a warm, open smile. For awhile we talked about women and Tibetan Buddhism, their training and their position in the Tibetan hierarchy of lamas. Very carefully and with great concern for my feelings, he explained that women get equal training, but do not seem to have the same desire for intense practice and study that the men show.

During a pause in the conversation, I asked, "Would there be one woman, to your knowledge, whom I could contact and perhaps even invite to Canada?" His Holiness became very thoughtful for awhile, then honestly admitted that he could not think of anyone, but said that he would make an inquiry.

Then I asked him if he had any ideas about how more women could be exposed to the Eight-Fold Path of Lord Buddha, the Compassionate One. Would it not help to spread this most peaceful gospel if more care and consideration were given to the education of young women in a Buddhist way of living? Women, as mothers, have the most powerful influence on the early years of their children. With this training they could do a much better job, which eventually could result in a greater contribution toward peace.

The Dalai Lama burst into happy laughter, "Yes, peace, harmony. Peace, we need this. I will look for a Tibetan nun for you. You write to me."

I asked carefully, "Should I address my letter to Mrs. Taring?" I had been in contact with her during my active years in the Tibetan Aid Society.

He objected, saying, "No, no. Write to me directly. I will get the letter, I assure you."

One of His Holiness' aides came and signalled that the next party were waiting for their appointment with him. We all rose and the Dalai Lama shook hands with us. I waited to be last because I had one more question. While he was holding my right hand, I took with my left a crystal mala from my neck, and looking straight into his eyes I asked, "Would you please put Tara's mantra into this mala?"

With another happy laugh he took the mala and went through six or eight beads, then put it back around my neck. Another cascade of laughter in which I joined with great joy, and then from the table he picked up the silken scarf that I had brought and offered to him, in the Tibetan tradition. He ran the scarf through his hands and around his neck and then put it around mine and tried to make a bow, all with happy laughter.

This exceptionally high mood affected everyone. His next words to me were, "Come and see me. Come to India. I will find a nun for you."

This gave me the courage to say that I had one more question. He laughingly replied, "What is it?"

Looking very intently at him, I said, "You are the fourteenth incarnation of the Dalai Lama. Is that correct?" He agreed. I am sure he was wondering what I was up to. And I felt I took him a bit by surprise by asking, "If there is no soul and no Self, what is it that incarnates?"

Another burst of laughter, and he threw his arms up, then became very serious and said, "I am standing here in front of you, and I am a man. And you are standing here and you are a woman. And at some time, we have been over there," and he gestured to his left. "Now we are here, and sometime we will be over there," gesturing to the right.

I was still not satisfied. I replied, "Your Holiness, if there is no 'we' and there are no selves, what is it that incarnated?" Then in the pause that followed I suggested, "Can we call it *essence*?"

His Holiness the fourteenth Dalai Lama. "His strong conviction, based on personal experience from long-standing spiritual practice and study, has made him the outstanding man that he is."

With some obvious feeling of relief, because he was not conversing in his own tongue, he laughingly agreed, "Yes, *essence* is a very good word. Let's call it essence."

One more handshake, and a last glance at the Tara picture on the pile of his business papers. Because the Dalai Lama must be inundated with correspondence, I hoped that by including the same image in future letters that he might remember me as the sender. The time for departure had come.

As I walked down the steps from the hotel to the car, I was wondering, as I felt the crystal mala on my body, how intimate my relationship to the Dalai Lama would be from now on. I felt there was no doubt of its seriousness, responsibility, and depth. I decided to see him in India; it was a matter of dates and preparation because of his timetable and my own.

The high spirit I left with remained with me for days to come.

The meager facts I had about the Dalai Lama as a person were supplemented by his book, *My Land and My People.* The Dalai Lama was born in the small village of Taktser in 1935, and was only sixteen years old when the situation in Tibet made it necessary for him to become head of government. He was filled with anxiety because he knew nothing of the world, and had no experience of politics. But even at his youthful age he recognized that as the Dalai Lama he was a symbol for his people, and the only person whom everyone would unanimously follow. What an experience it must have been: sixteen years old, facing the vast power of Communist China and an otherwise silent world that watched the spectacle without assisting.

Later in the biography the Dalai Lama describes his difficult decision to leave Tibet so he could to help his people from outside the borders by rallying international support. His flight from Tibet to India, with about one hundred people, was an arduous one through the Himalayas with the Chinese in pursuit. He himself was disguised as a soldier, complete with a rifle slung over his shoulder. And when at three o'clock one morning a dog barked near their place of hiding, all were holding their breath for fear of discovery.

His biographical account is in sharp contrast to the fantasies of many Westerners, some of whom profess to follow the Buddhist faith. Wild stories were circulated that the Dalai Lama had conjured by magic some mysterious clouds that hid him and his retinue from the sight of the Chinese. Did anyone ever think that soldiers, well-trained in warfare and full of ambition and eagerness to catch the God-king, would not be deterred by clouds? The Dalai Lama says, "There was nothing dramatic about our crossing the frontier. . . . I saw it in a daze of sickness and weariness and unhappiness, deeper than I can express."[1]

He also admits to enormous mental stress, as if he were standing between two volcanoes. Under this kind of pressure, which is hard to imagine for anyone who has never been in such a situation, what is there left to be done?

The strength of the Dalai Lama's faith is shown particularly when he speaks of his attitude towards death, and the prospect of being killed by his adversaries: "I felt then, as I always feel, that I am only a mortal being and an instrument of the never-dying spirit of my Master, and that the end of one mortal frame is not of any great consequence."[2]

---

[1] The Dalai Lama, *My Land and My People,* 216.

[2] Ibid. 195.

His strong conviction, based on personal experience from long-standing spiritual practice and study, has made him the outstanding man that he is. We speak of geniuses in the world of science, but it would be only just to say that the Dalai Lama is a genius in the spiritual field. I feel honored to have met him, and think that my destiny has been particularly kind to have brought this about. It is not the high office that he represents, or the God-king that he is to the Tibetan people that stirs a feeling of profound humility within me, but the greatness of character as a human being that I met in His Holiness, the Dalai Lama.

RESOURCES FOR THE READER

Suggested Reading

AVEDON, JOHN F. *An Interview With the Dalai Lama.* New York: Little-bird Publications, 1980.

THE DALAI LAMA. *My Life and My People: Memoirs of the Dalai Lama of Tibet.* New York: Potala Corporation, 1977.

THE DALAI LAMA. *Ocean of Wisdom: Guidelines for Living,* Clear Light Publishers, 1989.

THE DALAI LAMA. *The Opening of the Wisdom Eye and the History of the Advancement of Buddhadharma in Tibet. Wheaton:* Theosophical Publishing House, 1966.

CHAPTER *18*

SWAMI SIVANANDA

Although I have written an entire book on my guru, Swami Sivananda,[1] I wanted to add some reflections and insights I have gained over the years, to shed some additional light on the guru-disciple relationship and to show how a working relationship can extend over several lifetimes. It is only now, thirty-five years after my first meeting with him, that the pieces of the puzzle of our relationship are beginning to fall into place.

Years before meeting Gurudev Sivananda or consciously knowing anything about yoga or reincarnation, I had the following dream:

> Germany, 1948
>
> There was a beautiful temple with a flight of stairs leading to the water where a small boat was tied. I seemed to be wearing layers and layers of skirts. I was coming down the steps and I wanted to

[1] See *Radha: Diary of a Woman's Search.*

> leave to go to the other shore. But the moment I had my foot in the boat, a thundering voice called me back: "You can't leave yet—you haven't finished the job. If you go now, you'll be like someone sitting down at a table loaded with food, knowing that you've left starving people behind." Willingly, but with a heavy heart, I obeyed and climbed back up the steps.

I remember waking up from this dream experience with a very sad feeling, because I did not want to stay. I really wanted to go Home. But I also knew that this man, whom I interpreted to be the priest of the temple, had a point: I could not leave and have all the food (spiritual nourishment) just for myself, when other people were hungry (in need of the teachings).

The dream recurred several times over the years, becoming very strongly set in my memory and arousing my curiosity. Where was this temple? In what part of the world? Later, when I moved to England, I searched through many bookstores looking for some clue to the temple's architectural design, but found none. It was not Chinese, Japanese, or Indian. The temple remained alive in my heart, but an unsolved mystery in my mind.

In 1955, when I was first preparing to leave for India to meet Swami Sivananda, I thought, "Why am I not excited? Well, maybe when I am in the airplane. Maybe when I am in India. Maybe when I am at the ashram." When I met Gurudev Sivananda I was not nervous at all. Physically I came very close to him when I put my gift of the cross around his neck, yet still I wasn't nervous. I felt rather as if I was meeting him again, even though that feeling was astounding to me at the time.

Early in my stay Gurudev called me to him, to clear my doubts. He said, "You have been very close to me in previous births. Now you have come again. . . . I will reveal to you everything, but you must have patience. Wait."[2]

Shortly before I left India, in his farewell speech to me Sivananda repeated once more that we had lived together and worked together in a past life, so we have met here in this birth. He added that ". . . she already knows Yoga, only the Samskaras (impressions), which are

---

[2] Ibid. 55.

"You have been very close to me in previous births. Now you have come again . . . I will reveal to you everything, but you must have patience. Wait."

already engraved in her mind have to be brought back to the surface of consciousness."[3]

Soon after I had arrived at the ashram, Gurudev pointed to me, asking others, "Have you met this lady from Kashmir?" or, "Come over here and meet my friend from Kashmir." At the time, his remark seemed both pointless and silly to me, and I continued to find it odd until one day he introduced me to a couple from Kashmir, whom he had asked to come to the ashram with certain photographs. Sivananda was brimming with excitement as he told the man to show me the slides:

"There in the photograph was the temple that I had been trying to find for so long, a temple I had first seen years ago in a dream and later had come to me in meditation. Now I understood the joke that Master had made which I had thought was silly, "Meet my friend from Kashmir." So Gurudev had known all along of the experience I had had—obviously a past life experience that had taken place in Kashmir—and he had asked this couple to bring a photograph of the temple so that I would know it was real."[4]

At the time, the major impact of this incident was to shatter my old concepts of space and time. This was the temple from my dreams, and it was Sivananda who had arranged for for me to see these pictures. What if I *had* lived with him and worked with him in previous lifetimes?

Thirty years later I was telling this story to a group in Canada, and one of my associates mentioned that he had been to Kashmir. He then showed me photographs he had taken of a temple by the river, which to our amazement was the same temple. To find out more about this mysterious temple, he sent one of his photographs to the Indian High Commission with a request for any historical information.

Although at the ashram in India I had had the very definite and powerful feeling that this was *the* temple, later when I saw enlargements of his slides, I felt that although something was very familiar about the temple, it was also different from how I had experienced it.

The information that came back from the Indian government revealed why. Originally this temple had been a Kali temple, but in 1395 it had been redesigned and converted into a mosque.

A Kali temple! The idea resonated with a sense of familiarity, at the same time that it disturbed my rational mind. I had always felt a strong affinity to Kali and seemed to have an inherent understanding of her

---

[3] Ibid. 196.

[4] Ibid. 101–102.

"There in the photograph was the temple that I had been trying to find for so long, a temple I had first seen years ago in a dream and later had come to me in meditation."

symbolism. I remembered back to the early 1960s when I had been given a mala of skulls carved out of ivory, which I wore only occasionally because it was somewhat unsettling to others. Kali, of course, is typically depicted wearing a garland of skulls.

Next to the present mosque was something that looked like a miniature temple building. This building, they said, was still used by worshippers of Kali even today.

The past began falling more and more convincingly into the present for me.

I remembered back to India and one day asking Gurudev, "Are there any other Sivanandas?"

"Yes, there was a Sivananda who was the president of the Ramakrishna Order; he died several years ago." And then with a facial expression of dismissal, as if to say, "Don't ask me any more," he said, "The other Sivanandas were in Kashmir."

This didn't help me too much at the time but I tucked it away, realizing that there was some importance to it.

Thirty-five years later, I was given some Kashmiri texts that had been translated for the first time, and I read about the other Sivanandas in Kashmir.[5] The first Sivananda lived from the beginning to middle of the ninth century A.D. and was said to be the first exponent of the Krama school of Kashmiri yoga. It is known that he received the teachings from a female preceptor, unidentified except as "the yogini," and that his three major disciples were women. A second Sivananda lived in the early to middle part of the twelfth century and was a major influence on the thinking of his time.

In these same texts with the information on the Kashmiri Sivanandas, I found many references to the Light.[6] For the first time I saw phrases being used that I had used for many, many years—*the light of understanding, the light of consciousness, bringing light into the heart*—and descriptions of experiences I had received through the Light Invocation—the body as a spiritual tool and the body as a mass of Light. For years I had researched various scriptures and their translations: Was there anything about the Divine Light Invocation?[7] Light was very often

---

[5] See Rastogi, *Krama Tantrism of Kashmir.*

[6] See Dyczkowski, *The Doctrine of Vibration.*

[7] See Radha, *The Divine Light Invocation.* The Light and the Devine Light Invocation are key images and practices in Swami Radha's teachings.

mentioned, but I had never come across the Light Invocation in its fullness until, in 1990, I was presented with these Kashmiri teachings.

It took a long time before I could relate in my present life, to the events in the past. In the beginning, the incidents gave me a theoretical understanding that what survives death is a vortex of energy, which we normally call "consciousness," and which will keep in its memory only those things that are significant.

I thought that perhaps people escape into the *theory* of reincarnation, because the experience that in another life we have actually been another person, and perhaps sometime a person we would rather not have been, is too frightening. As kings or queens we may have killed many people, or ordered many people to kill others. We may have been at war or may have satisfied our greed at the cost of life and suffering to many others.

Then I began to understand another side of it—that at one time we may have accepted an assignment that could stretch over many lifetimes. The idea of the Bodhisattva as one who will come again and again "to do the job," can contribute to this understanding. This is not our usual Western image of the Bodhisattva as some supernatural being who is both visible and invisible, and wears flowing robes, and so on, but rather is someone who takes birth every now and then, with a very particular purpose—not necessarily to do what the personality aspects want to do.

I had several experiences with healing at Sivananda Ashram but Gurudev said to me, "No, that is not your mission. You have to update the teachings." Of course it would be much more attention-catching to heal others, but if that was not my mission, I had better not do it.

By sitting quietly and letting things come to us, sometimes we will know what we could do and what we should do. And we will see that we are capable of doing what we *ought* to do; but most people just don't want to do it. In fact what we *want* to do is often the biggest barrier to our development. But if we really want to know what we should do in our lives, the first step is to reflect on the important parts in this life, and question again and again, Why was I born? What is the purpose of my life?

The greatest lesson that I learned from Swami Sivananda's lack of explanation about our past together, was the necessity for my personal experience and my personal search. If I really wanted to find out, I would. I do remember that in India, Gurudev would sometimes ask me enigmatic questions that I could not answer, perhaps hoping that I would remember something of this past. But he was very careful not to reveal too much, because it has to be one's *own* experience.

I have often said that I am not a Hindu, I am a practicing yogini. That is still the best description. Yoga is the path of knowledge that permitted me to find the Light within myself, and to discover my own divinity. Gurudev Sivananda, a man of great character, was my inspiration in awakening to this Light.

RESOURCES FOR THE READER

Suggested Reading

DYCZKOWSKI, MARK S. G. *The Canon of the Saivagama and the Kubjika Tantras of the Western Kaula Tradition.* New York: State University of New York Press, 1988.

DYCZKOWSKI, MARK S. G. *The Doctrine of Vibration.* New York: State University of New York Press, 1987.

MULLER-ORTEGA, PAUL EDUARDO. *The Triadic Heart of Siva.* New York: State University of New York Press, 1989.

RADHA, SWAMI SIVANANDA. *Radha: Diary of a Woman's Search.* 2d ed Palo Alto: Timeless Books, 1990.

RASTOGI, NAVJIVAN. *Krama Tantricism of Kashmir.* Vol. 1. Delhi: Motilal Banarsidass, 1979.

SIVANANDA, SWAMI. *Concentration and Meditation.* Sivananda Nagar, Rishikesh: Divine Life Society, 1955.

SIVANANDA, SWAMI. *Lord Krishna: His Lilas and Teachings.* Rishikesh: Divine Life Society, 1981.

SIVANANDA, SWAMI. *Sure Ways for Success in Life and God-Realization.* Sivananda Nagar, Rishikesh: Divine Life Society, 1977.

SIVANANDA, SWAMI. *Tantra Yoga, Nada Yoga, and Kriya Yoga.* Rishikesh: Divine Life Society, 1955.

SIVANANDA, SWAMI. *Voice of the Himalayas.* Rishikesh: Divine Life Society, 1953.

Sivananda's Ashram

Divine Life Society, Sivanandanagar, 249 192 U.P. India

CHAPTER 19

COLLECTING THE NECTAR

Meeting all these spiritual leaders, I often felt like a bee collecting nectar from many flowers. From each teacher I gathered inspiration that influenced my life and helped me carry out the work my own guru, Swami Sivananda, set before me.

Sivananda believed that "selfless service will make you divine." His whole ashram operated on that basis. In the beginning of his spiritual life, Gurudev was a bhakta, expressing devotion in worship of Radha and Krishna, the divine lovers. In later years he became a Vedantin, but his was a practical wisdom that allowed no time for fruitless speculation. The daily reflection he stressed had a very practical purpose: "I made this mistake today; how could I have done things better?" This character development was worked out through the daily Karma Yoga of the ashram. I have used the same principles in my own life and applied them at Yasodhara Ashram: be considerate, do the work as an offering to the Divine, and put quality into every action. Theory is not enough; the lesson must be put into practice to have any value.

At his ashram Gurudev would distribute cookies and sweets, chocolates, biscuits, and lots of fruit. He always had something special in his pockets for the children, and a few rupees to give to poor villagers—he was very generous in that way. I remember that he personally gave out pullovers to those who had no warm clothes for the winters in the Himalayan foothills. His words to me, "Be a spiritual mother to all," were backed by his own example. His care and generosity made him an exception among Eastern gurus, and this aspect of his character has been an inspiration and reminder to me over the years. However, he was very different with his time for people, and was not easily accessible either to new aspirants or to long-time disciples.

Papa Ramdas, on the other hand, was accessible to everybody. I often was able to talk with him for several hours and could ask him any question on points that needed clarifying. But if he had cookies, he kept the box under lock and key, and when he did open it, he would hand the cookies out carefully, like prasad. Papa was very thrifty with material things, but gave freely of his time and wisdom. He gave me details of the legal setup of the ashram as well as a complete list of his American devotees to contact. From our discussions on the administration of his ashram, I was able to gather much practical advice on setting up Yasodhara Ashram in Canada. Papa's humility was outstanding, and his words, "You hold onto me, Ram, when I can't hold onto you," have echoed in me during times of great challenge over the years.

Another rich source of spiritual nourishment for me was my Tibetan guru, the man who taught me so much but whose Tibetan name was so hard to pronounce. On my last visit to him, I asked him to spell his name for me so that I could write it down, but he waved off my request saying, "We meet in the heart. I like the name you have given me. Stay with that." His technique for smashing concepts was frightening, yet gave a sense of exhilarating freedom. His teaching focused on developing the powers of the mind, yet his requirement for devotion and obedience made him a disciplinarian of a high order. He also showed me how pain is self-created through uncontrolled emotions, imagination, and ideas about perfection.

Many of the Tibetan guru's teachings are incorporated into my book *Kundalini Yoga for the West.* Rigorous self-questioning and clarification of concepts have proven to be most powerful methods in my own life, and tools that the Western mind can grasp.

Swami Purushottamananda was able to see the divinity in all, and he certainly transmitted a taste of that tranquillity to me. Through his influence I was shown levels of awareness that I had not known existed. Although his teaching was conveyed partly through speech, it was also accomplished by the powers of the mind or through thought transmission. Subtle discoveries based on our encounter have kept emerging over the years. It is not possible to put into words his effect on me, or my gratitude. Sweeping statements would be true but not sufficient.

Meeting women who were powerful spiritual leaders was particularly meaningful for me, as a woman. Much of my own work has been aimed at encouraging other women to realize their potential; and though the conditioning is often so strong that the task seems impossible at times, those women who are willing to take responsibility for themselves and can move toward emotional independence, are most precious. They create the needed examples for others to follow.

Two of the women saints I met, Mother Krishna Bai and Anandamayi Ma, while different, pursued the same path. Since neither knew English, I could speak to them only through interpreters. For me, the lack of oral communication was an asset, because it meant I truly had to listen, surrendering all my mental activities to allow hearing in depth. Anandamayi Ma and Mother Krishna Bai enticed a sensitivity or tuning in on the level of intuitive perception. Both women, with their practical wisdom and inspirational qualities, created an impact through their presence alone.

Anandamayi Ma's daily offering to me of an hour of her meditation time was a generous confirmation and support that nurtured my heart's desire through difficult times. In a similar way, the leader of Kailas Ashram also offered to recite a daily mala for me for a year, and presented me with the roses from Divine Mother's worship.

Such offerings touched me deeply and increased my confidence. A self-doubting part of my mind thought Gurudev was just being nice to me, and that I really wasn't strong enough to meet the challenge he had set before me. But here were spiritual teachers whom I hardly knew, who also seemed aware of my purpose and wanted to assist me spiritually. I often follow their example by giving gifts of spiritual practice to sincere aspirants facing new challenges on their paths; and I encourage my students to give spiritual gifts of mantra or Divine Light Invocations to others, because they are the most valuable gifts we can offer.

To cultivate devotion and the finer feelings of gratitude and humility is sometimes difficult for the Western mind, which tends to worship the intellect. But the path of the heart is a direct path to the heart of the Divine. My brief interaction with the shankaracharya of Kanchi was a good warning for me to restrain my need to examine and question whenever it might interfere with the simple faith of others.

Meher Baba was an excellent example of living devotion. His incredible demonstration of love toward all people, regardless of their appearance or condition, inspired a desire in me to penetrate the outer form to the essence within every person. The practice of seeing myself in the Light and visualizing whomever I am talking with wrapped in Light, has helped me to maintain contact with the highest level in each individual. Students whom I train to teach have first to master this ability to contact the best in the other, by keeping their focus on the Light or mantra.

Ramakrishna, whom I met in spirit while visiting his ashram, helped me to keep this focus and perspective. His laughing response to my personality's worries reminded me to distinguish between my two selves, and echoed Gurudev's words, "Think of yourself always as Radha, and you can do anything." When we identify with Divine Mother, we become Divine Mother or at least one of her little sparks; that is the proper identification. When we identify with the Light, we become the Light. The affirmation, "I am not the body. I am not the mind. I am Light eternal," can help dissolve wrongly placed self-importance and fears, and remind us to return to the wisdom within.

Although I never met Sarada Devi, she had a strong influence on me nevertheless. I was especially inspired by her practice of going to the rooftop and calling her spiritual children home, so I followed her example. I would lift up my arms, like in the Divine Light Invocation, and say to Divine Mother, "I am here. Send anyone I can help."

Two outstanding bhaktis, Dilip Kumar Roy and Indira Devi, were also spiritual leaders who put their devotion into action. Theirs was a remarkable combination of spiritual gifts: Indira, with her longing for the Divine, heard the songs of Krishna in her meditation; and Dilip, through his musical genius, was able to recreate the songs that Indira could bring back only in part. Their evening satsangs were open to those who wished to listen to Mira's songs and to Dilip's discourse on the Gita, which always referred to the need for a pure and worshipful heart. Their faith was such that they allowed the messages of Princess Mira to direct their lives. Such words and songs, composed to glorify the Divine as perceived by the worshipper, provide one of the safest paths to Realization.

My own instruction into the intricacies of Indian music was given by three men who were masters in their fields. Professor Shastri gave me some understanding of the power of sound and the effect of vibrations on the human body. Swami Nadabrahmananda, whom I consider my music guru, was able to demonstrate the theories in practice. He also taught me mantras and bhajans, and how to play a number of musical instruments. Gopalacharya showed me the fluctuations and variations with which mantras could be chanted, and how the energy of emotions could be turned from a destructive to constructive direction through chanting.

Mantra is a cornerstone of my teachings, and after experiencing the effects of these methods and suggestions, I have since passed on the instructions of my three music teachers to many Western students. The refinement of emotions into true feelings is a necessary step in spiritual development, and mantra is the key that opens the door to the Highest.

Dance, too, when performed as an offering to the Divine, provides a way to refine and redirect the emotions. Through devotional dance, the body can become a moving prayer. From Mr. Devasatyam I was able to learn six dances in a month, and to see that each Indian dance has its own spiritual message whose significance is clearly expressed. Although Mr. Devasatyam never demonstrated, his explanations were so precise that Gurudev was pleased with the accuracy of my movements. My experience with Indian dance so clearly showed me the potential of the body as a spiritual tool, that I now encourage my own students to practice the subtle dance movements with the focus on devotion rather than technique.

Each of the spiritual teachers I met had something to give, and each knew the price of knowledge. The sadhu whom I met with Ayyapan, concretely demonstrated a subtle psychological principle. His explanation for throwing stones at people—to separate the sincere from the merely curious—is one I have put into practice metaphorically in the workshops over the years. Who could withstand assaults on their egos and not run away frightened or resentful? Those were the people who, by their courage, showed me they were not just curiosity-seekers, but were willing to pay the price for knowledge.

But what is meant by knowledge? At Sadhu Vaswani's schools, where I taught for several weeks, I heard three-year-olds reciting Gita verses—clearly demonstrating to me that familiarity with the scriptures is no sign of spiritual wisdom. Texts can be recited without any understanding whatsoever. The teenage girls at the school were surprised that a foreigner would be interested in their culture, and even more surprised that such a person could interpret the ancient texts. I explained that because the teachings are presented symbolically, they have a wide range of possible meanings; to be of value now, the heart of their meaning must be made relevant to our own time. The focus of my work has been to update the ancient teachings, extracting their wisdom and making them accessible and practical guides.

Another approach to knowledge was granted to me through my interviews with Phra Bimaladharma, the head of all Buddhists in Thailand. I was able not only to discuss with him many points of Buddhist philosophy, but from my experience of walking between the aisles of Buddhas, I later developed the "Straight Walk" workshop. This method brings to the Westerner the experience of the Eastern ideal of mindfulness, of maintaining awareness with every step taken.

My short time with another Buddhist, the Dalai Lama, confirmed to me his strong character. My attempt to understand the Buddhist view of "what incarnates" if there is no soul or atman, resulted in our tentative agreement on the term *essence. Soul* is so over-used and loaded with different connotations that I preferred to find a word more descriptive and open to exploration. Most people have made very few attempts to really discover this essence or soul force within themselves, whatever name they give it. One way that I start aspirants thinking and questioning is to have them draw a symbol for their essence in the "Life Seal" workshop. The picture is a good reflection of their degree of self-knowledge, and can be used to guide them to the next step—if they are willing to take it.

Unfortunately, many who start on the spiritual path are not willing to pay the price for knowledge, through their own efforts and perseverance. Sai Baba's teaching, "Is it the fault of the tree that all the flowers do not turn to fruit?" was a great help to me in seeing the limits of my responsibility for students who dropped away over the years. His words helped ease my concerns that I might have missed something, or not understood, or not met the needs of students whose choice and karma led them away from their spiritual promise.

Having a Western saint, Padre Pio, confirm to me in such a clear and remarkable way that all Truth is one—that the wisdom of the East is not different from the wisdom of the West—seemed to add a special blessing to my work of making the Eastern teachings accessible to the Western world.

The most important gift that I received from all the gurus I met was their encouragement to escalate my mental powers and understanding. While the responsibility is awesome and somewhat frightening, it seems to me that the purpose of life is to develop the mind, to overcome limitations, and to continue to increase awareness of Consciousness.

In the Western world we have our own gurus. They are the politicians, financiers, and scientists who influence public thought, some of whose friends and subordinates regard them as "gurus" in a very personal and specific sense. Sorensen, for example, felt this way about Kennedy and even said, "Everything I know I learned from him."[1]

As with the Eastern gurus, some are dedicated, concerned human beings, but some are ruthless opportunists. We must use our awareness and discrimination to decide whether or not they deserve our trust. If they deceive us, it is because we have allowed ourselves to be deceived.

This puts the responsibility right back on ourselves. What do we want to open ourselves up to? What do we want to take in? We can use the analogy of food that can nourish the body when taken in measured, well-balanced quantities, and so contributes to good health. What do we feed the mind? Fantasies of the ego-mind that are destructive and may even cost us our lives? Or will we be inspired to go in search of the nectar, the essence, and find our true citizenship, not of our country, our world, or even the universe, but of the Light? The foremost duty for us, as human beings endowed with consciousness, is to go in search of knowledge and higher values in life.

RESOURCES FOR THE READER

Suggested Reading—Swami Sivananda Radha

RADHA, SWAMI SIVANANDA. *The Divine Light Invocation.* 3d ed. Palo Alto: Timeless Books, 1990.

---

[1] Says Sorensen today, "Everything I know I learned from him. He had the brains, the personality, the patience, the eloquence, the high standards, the dedication. I learned to have confidence, to be honest and candid. I learned caution. The list is endless. He was always the same. When things were bad, he knew they would get better. When things were great, he knew they could get worse."

To Sorensen, who generally shuns superlatives, Kennedy was a kind of cosmic accident: a combination of qualities that one man rarely possesses, and the man was in the right place at the right time. The years in the White House were to Ted Sorensen "a golden age." Right to the last it was hard for him to realize that he had, finally, to leave it.

"I never thought I would have to make that decision," he reflects. "It is the best job in the world. The White House is the best place in the world to work. It is the most important and worthwhile work."

The above quote is an example of the guru-disciple relationship in politics, with the disciple lavish in praise of the guru.

"Sorensen," *Life,* March 6, 1964.

RADHA, SWAMI SIVANANDA. *Hatha Yoga: The Hidden Language.* Porthill: Timeless Books, 1989.

RADHA, SWAMI SIVANANDA. *Kundalini Yoga for the West.* Spokane: Timeless Books, 1978.

RADHA, SWAMI SIVANANDA. *Mantras: Words of Power.* Porthill: Timeless Books, 1980.

RADHA, SWAMI SIVANANDA. *Radha: Diary of a Woman's Search.* 2d ed Palo Alto: Timeless Books, 1990.

Swami Radha's Centers

CANADA

Yasodhara Ashram, Box 9, Kootenay Bay, B.C., Canada V0B 1X0 (contact the Ashram for addresses of other centers across Canada)

UNITED STATES

Publishing Division: Timeless Books, P.O. Box 50905, Palo Alto, CA. 94303-0673

A.D.H.P. (Association for Development of Human Potential) House, West 2328 Pacific Ave., Spokane, WA 99204

GREAT BRITAIN

Radha House, 7 Roper Road, Canterbury, Kent, England CT2 7EH

Part TWO

Reflecting the Light

Chapter 20

Aspiration~ Spiritual Learning

What propels a person to become a spiritual aspirant? Why should one aspire to something more than is already present? For some people it may be an urge to find more meaning in life—an empty place needs to be filled or a stagnant life enriched. For others it may suddenly be imperative to find the purpose in life, especially if pleasures have lost their impact or the price has become too high for their short duration. Sometimes the reason for the seeking is unknown, and it may even feel like groping in the dark.

While dissatisfaction with life is often a starting point for spiritual life, it is seldom a sufficient driving force to catapult seekers toward the goal of Self-Realization. What is needed is a willingness to learn, a passionate desire for knowledge, and an intense yearning to evolve toward the Light.

If we use our intelligence correctly, which means with discrimination, we can learn from anyone and everyone. Whenever we listen and observe, we can learn, even from a dog, or from an ant carrying a weight many times her own. So if we are willing to acquire knowledge by these kinds of efforts, we also open ourselves to greater wisdom that follows. We attract this wisdom and we begin to see it everywhere.

When we really want to learn, we have to accept the opportunities any way they come to us. If I am critical of someone's bad habit, I have to learn not to imitate it. So I can learn even what not to do, which is perhaps the first part of the learning process. On the other hand, if someone shows certain strengths in conducting herself, I will ask, "Why do you do it this way?" So again, because I want to learn, I will make myself the inquirer and pick out what I recognize is best for me at each stage of my development.

But we can only learn according to our ability to surrender pre-judgments and preconceived ideas. The mechanicalness in our behavior that has been established almost from the time we were born, has to be changed. We have to clarify why we think every single thought, why we do every single action in daily life, because only then can we become aware of how conditioned we are.

By clarifying, "Where do I imitate my father, my mother, or any authority in my life?" and by deciding "I want to be my own person," then I can start to become my own person. But if I still live by the values of the past, I cannot. If I am not my own person, I have no freedom and will never learn to handle freedom.

The unconscious can be compared to a bowl. If this bowl is already filled with preconceived ideas from past experiences and training, then what else can be put into it? So the old must be recognized and cleared out, if it has no value. This creates space for new insights and new intuitions, which are no longer overruled by past judgment or condemnation.

All the residue in the deeper levels of the mind has to be removed somehow. It is like a salty crust at the bottom of the bowl that has to be dissolved and washed away by a flow of clear, fresh water. Involvement with the Divine is this fresh water. People often say they want to be a channel for something higher; then they have to be a well-scrubbed channel. Otherwise they are like a rusty pipe: along with the water comes the debris.

One day Swami Sivananda poured me a cup of coffee and asked me to go outside with him. Then he began to pour milk into the coffee. Of course the coffee overflowed with the milk, and there was less and less coffee, until eventually there was just a hint of coffee color in the milk. The coffee symbolizes the negative aspects, and it is only by pouring in the milk of divine wisdom that we will finally remove all the darkness, not by analyzing how the coffee got there. But for those who cannot pour the milk in, then analyzing how the coffee got there is the only other way, but it is a hard way.

Many people are victims of self-deception, thinking they have gained knowledge when they have only acquired information. We have to test our knowing in our own lives. We cannot take for granted that our knowledge is all inspiration, and we cannot believe anything without trying it out. We want to be persons of knowledge, not believers or collectors of information.

Sivananda would sometimes say, "Look at all the pundits. They squabble about splitting hairs but they don't give a drink of pure, clear water to those who come to them thirsting." Pride in the intellect and focus on the mental aspects keep aspirants from true contact with themselves and the right kind of worship. Love, devotion, and humility are not acquired by reading, writing, or reciting, but by daily living.

The distance between life in the world and spiritual life is not that great. Life is the battlefield of the Gita. If you put quality into your daily life you will put quality into your spiritual life. But if you have no inner desire for quality, except as a means to gather compliments, then you will have no real quality in your life. It is like someone who cooks marvelously, not because he wants people to be well and healthy, but to have praise for what a good cook he is. That is the wrong motive, from a spiritual point of view.

What is most important for any aspirant is to develop a constant focus on the Divine. This can be achieved through using a number of methods: sometimes focusing on the feeling of presence, sometimes on the thought, sometimes on an image, sometimes having an internal or even external dialogue with the Divine, as if the Divine were another person. But in the beginning the focus has to be quite definite, so you don't fool yourself by saying, "I'm going to the beach—that's where I will find God." Of course once you are there, you will not concentrate on the Divine but will be distracted by the clouds, the boats, the people, the activities. There has to be a willingness to look at the facts without indulging in illusions.

Your relationship with the Divine has to be like a love affair between a man and a woman. If he is working and she has told him she will meet him at five o'clock, he thinks of this all day: "Oh, it's not five yet. Now it's lunch break, it's getting closer." These are very fleeting and subtle thoughts, but they are there. If those thoughts can be for the Divine, then when you meet, it will be even more pleasurable than meeting with your beloved. By personalizing the Divine in this way, the emotions are also satisfied. The emotions, which need this satisfaction for a long time, are given what they need rather than being beaten down, and gradually they will become less and less greedy until the power that they express has been subdued and moved into the heart. Then will come the knowing of the heart.

Commitment to the Divine is essential. Never, never give up on that. Just as you don't like to be let down, don't let the Divine down. Think of the Divine as your best friend. Don't dwell too much on your personal problems, but instead consider how you can focus more clearly on the Divine. Establish a magnet in yourself that will draw the Divine to you. By creating that magnet in your own mind, you will attract divine intuition and the Divine in other people.

The only abstract way of being in contact with the Divine is by thinking that, even in the darkest moments, you are walking in the Light. In order to get that constant focus, you have to strip yourself of unnecessary mental clutter.

Eventually you have to do for the Divine out of love for the Divine. But then you have to clarify what you mean. People often hear that, "If I love God, then I am a good person. So yes, I love God." But they do not even know what they are supposed to love. Can you love something unknown? Every seeker needs to take time for this kind of reflection. When reflection is carried out for a long time, then meditation will come in a natural way. But most people who try meditating first, don't get very far.

In the beginning we are all spiritual babies. And like babies, our walk is not very steady. We toddle from one side to the other. We fall. We have to get up and try again. But eventually we have to grow up and mature, so that those divine forces, by whatever name we call them, can really work through us.

When we do reach a certain stage of maturity, then a guru is needed, not to cater to dependency, but simply because the guru knows what the aspirant does not know but wants to learn. The guidance of a guru can be very important in assuring that certain spiritual practices are not done prematurely and that the necessary self-investigation and groundwork are carried out. When you practice spiritual exercises, you are dealing with the precious instrument of the human mind. You can experiment on your own, but then you risk having unpleasant accidents. It is like discovering loose wires hanging down and not knowing if they are live or not. Will they give you a shock? Will it be just a little shock or will it go right through your body and kill you? You need somebody who knows.

You can accept inspirations from the guru, but these inspirations have to serve as the arrows that will carry your own thoughts to the target. If the guru's words are not taken in, explored from your own perspective, and acted on, then listening to a guru is nothing but a different kind of entertainment that won't make you a better person at all. You have to do the work yourself.

If we think of the guru as a spiritual genius, then the aspirant is a genius in the making. At the beginning, the potential genius does not necessarily have a clear picture of the heights that can be achieved. There is just an inner knowing, undefined by the mind. By persevering in the search, escalation to ever-greater heights is possible.

Chapter 21

The Guru~ A Spiritual Genius?

A guru who truly deserves to be called a saint, I would rather call a genius in the spiritual field, since the word *saint* has so many fantasies attached to it. We can regard a spiritual genius in the same light as any other person who has achieved very high levels in his or her particular field.

To have developed potentials to an extraordinary extent requires constant searching—never taking anything for granted, never accepting any limit, and transcending firmly established thoughts, beliefs, and assumptions. The secret of any genius is a deep-rooted, unwavering commitment to what has been envisioned. Think how many musicians there are, and how very few are geniuses. How many conservatories are there on just the American continent, and how many students have even tried to become professionals? How many of these have become musical geniuses?

Bach, a musical genius, wrote magnificent music without any conscious knowledge of the laws of harmony. Leonardo da Vinci was a genius of artistic mastery and inventive creativity far ahead of his time. Unlike these other geniuses, the guru is not an inventor or originator, but an experiencer and transmitter of the spiritual teachings. All such spiritual geniuses are very humble, being fully aware that they are only instruments for the Divine Will. They do not consider themselves superior beings, but only translators of the spiritual language they have learned.

The enlightened guru has extraordinary knowledge—not the theoretical knowledge of the scholar, but eternal knowledge that has come through intuitive perception. The spiritual genius is aware of many sources of knowledge that are not available to everybody (or even to those who want to know), and has become a magnet for attracting this knowledge.

The guru's field is the expansion of consciousness. Leonardo da Vinci explored certain laws and overcame them in his way. Einstein had tremendously innovative ideas, but he probably did not have the knowledge of how to expand consciousness. Sometimes when people speak as if the kundalini experience is a common, everyday occurrence, I ask, "Do you think Leonardo da Vinci had kundalini? Do you think Einstein had kundalini?" If these men, who are considered geniuses, had not fully expanded their personal consciousness, then how can so many ordinary people have done so? The purpose of the true guru is to expand personal consciousness and to help others do the same.

Can any genius foresee what will happen to what he or she has discovered? The powers that are loosed are neutral, and therefore only a few who follow will remember if they are acting in the spirit of the discovery. Perhaps Einstein would not have revealed his theory of relativity had he foreseen that its application would create the threat of total destruction. The guru, too, has to be very careful with the power of knowledge, because some disciples whose aim is self-glorification, will misuse the teachings and even distort them.

Just as the scientific genius isn't necessarily a musical genius, or the genius in chemistry isn't knowledgeable about every branch of chemistry and isn't necessarily a wonderful person as well, it is similar with the genius in the spiritual field. Westerners often think that if you have a state of enlightenment you can answer questions like, "How many molecules are in that table?" or, "What would be the best chemical mixture to achieve this result?" Some people can answer such questions, but they are not necessarily enlightened. If the guru is not interested in such information, then his or her knowledge also will be of a very different kind.

People often make the mistake of thinking that if their personalities are well-balanced and if they are very "good," then they are spiritual. Swami Sivananda would say they are do-gooders. If I follow the Light, I may have walked out of the darkness and left the spider webs behind. I may not have cleaned up the spider webs, if that was not my concern. I may not care to be nice to others so that they will think nicely of me, because that also may not be my concern.

Being nice is no indication of spiritual knowledge. There are some bhaktis who may be useless in practical life and may have very unpleasant personalities, but still they are absorbed in the Divine. Chaitanya, a fifteenth-century guru, certainly did not have a pleasant personality, but his thinking was constantly on Radha and Krishna. He had such a bad temper that sometimes he took a stick and cracked it down on the heads of his disciples. Because he had a terrible temper did not mean he was was not a spiritual genius. If your love for the Divine is great, the Divine accepts you with all your faults, and you will influence those around you anyway, whether you have a pleasant personality or not.

Pleasantness and attempts to be an easy person to live with can be a bonus, but they are only part of the personality make-up of an individual and cannot be demanded of everyone. And if my purpose is to stay focused on the Light, then who cares whether anyone likes me? The desire to be liked can be a distraction from my goal. It is not important to become a perfect person. It is enough to gain awareness of my actions, to know the repercussions and to decide which repercussions I would rather not have, but without losing sight of the final goal.

Traditionalists believe a spiritual genius can emerge only from a whole line of gurus. Whether or not there is a line of gurus doesn't really matter, because nobody invents anything totally new. Every religion is built on another. Let us remember that the Buddha built on the foundation of ancient Hindu beliefs and that Christ expanded on the Hebraic tradition.

The tradition of the gurus goes back to the ancient rishis, from whom the inspiration for the teachings first came. A philosophical system was developed around the original ideas, and was expanded over the years into a whole school of thought. If we look back to the rishis and the ancient gurus, whose purpose was to bring their disciples to a higher level of consciousness, we can see the thread of tradition that is carried on by the true guru of today.

But we still have to ask, "What was going on in the mind of the seer?" Even the greatest message passes through a human mind and is tainted by it. That is why each individual has to be encouraged to have his or her own experiences. My experience can only stimulate others to find their own, because the description of any experience is formulated through the language of the human mind.

It must also be remembered that no rishi, no guru, no prophet or spiritual genius is always in a state of bliss or constant communion with the Divine. Swami Sivananda was a great teacher but I have also seen his human weaknesses. The weaknesses did not irritate me because I could separate them from the teachings. I did not go to India to watch his human weaknesses emerge; I went because he had something I wanted, and I stayed for that. If you want to learn how to build a beautiful cabinet and you go to the best cabinetmaker in town and he teaches you, and then you discover by going there again and again, that he is quarrelling with his wife, would you now judge him to be a bad cabinetmaker? No. You are not concerned about the quarrels with his wife. You want from him what he has—his skill as a cabinetmaker.

To know that even a spiritual genius has a human side is very important. In the New Testament, the one story that shows this human side of Jesus is when he cracked the whip among the moneychangers in front of the temple. When I read this story, I thought, "If he is the Son of God, then why did he have to crack the whip? Why didn't he *enlighten* their minds?" Then I could see that the human personality of Jesus knew that the whip would be the only language they understood. Divine revelations would not have worked with their level of awareness. If any gurus or spiritual geniuses, including Jesus or the Buddha, were without human aspects then they could make no demands of others, because they would have no knowledge of what it means to be human.

Sivananda knew this very well. When I told him my self-doubts, that I wasn't really as good as he thought, and that he didn't know all I had done or thought in my life, he said, "You have to have your own stomach ulcers to know what that means." So you have to have suffered to understand human suffering and pain. You have to have made mistakes in order to develop compassion.

It is a Western idea to think that if consciousness is expanded, then there is absolute harmony in all situations. That is looking for emotional satisfaction. Politicians who emotionally satisfy the general public can do anything and still be acceptable, without making any valuable contribution to their country. In the same way, pseudo-gurus satisfy the emotional greed of their followers by giving them what they want, rather than challenging them to take steps toward Higher Consciousness.

There cannot be a single standard to determine "Who is an enlightened guru?" or "Who is a spiritual genius?" because ten people will have ten different judgments; the assessment depends on the perceiver's state of development. Enlightenment has as many levels as awareness.

Rather than try to assess the guru's level of enlightenment, it is more advisable for seekers to assess themselves. The degree of one's own self-knowledge and understanding gives a good measure of the degree of enlightenment. For those who are motivated and who put in the effort to learn and evolve, eventually this self-understanding will become more than a psychological knowing, and there will develop an openness to divine inspiration. By making themselves accessible to higher knowledge, seekers, too, may come to reflect the eternal wisdom that is radiating from other sources.

CHAPTER 22

ASHRAMS~ CENTERS OF LIGHT

When a devotee has a love affair with the Divine, the experience may create a desire for a spiritual and secluded life. Yet the intensity of his or her devotion can produce an indescribable quality that attracts others, as a light attracts moths. In this natural way, a group may gather around the one who has something to give, thereby forming the nucleus of an ashram.

Some ashrams also come into being when the guru sees the need for more centers to disseminate knowledge. Other ashrams arise at the instigation of followers, who may grow so numerous that they require more living space in order to stay with the guru.

When the number of followers grows, bringing the need for more and more material things such as housing, food, and storage, then regulations come into being and the ashram becomes an institution. It is similar to a family that, although it started with a husband and wife as lovers, becomes an institution with the arrival of children.

Ashrams differ as much as the gurus who founded them. While Sivananda Ashram and the Ramakrishna Order were often brimming with people, and there were often a hundred people a night at Dilip Kumar Roy's satsang hall, Purushottamananda allowed only one or two disciples to be with him, and this not even on a regular basis.

But in any ashram there is room for only one school of thought. Even though there may be value in other doctrines, a focus is needed for the teachings to be most effective. That may seem to contradict the theory of oneness, and be confusing to the Westerner who assumes that oneness, particularly the Vedantic viewpoint, can be applied to all situations. But focus is necessary so that each student can gain a deep understanding of one system, rather than let the mind be entertained by many possibilities.

Those who live at an ashram should be there to further their spiritual growth. Youthful enthusiasm brings people to ashrams and monasteries, often to stay for quite a few years in the hope of being made into saints. In that time something may rub off on them that will be of benefit later in life, but no one can be made into a saint; one must want to be a saint, to become one. There has to be the desire for the Divine, which also means the willingness to deal with one's ego and self-will.

Some people live with one foot only in the religious setting and the other still in the world. This division inevitably leads to deep emotional trouble, since such people are neither here nor there, in their personal relationships or in their work situations. The little understood saying in the Old Testament "I, the Lord thy God, am a jealous God" means that if you have committed yourself to the Lord, then "I, the Lord, will jealously hold onto you." We cannot serve two masters.

Centers that are run in a regimented, highly disciplined way are necessary for those who do not have the ability to direct their self-will into the right channels. Procrastination, resulting from lack of self-discipline, can be almost an addiction in some students. Reliance and dependency on the guru who provides the needed control is often sharply criticized outside the community, without taking into consideration that the majority of people do not have the ability to handle greater freedom.

However, the guru whose path is Bhakti Yoga or Karma Yoga becomes an example for his or her followers. Pleasing the guru through service is often the first motivation for the aspirant to strive to do a job

A view of Sivananda Ashram in Rishikesh, on the banks of the holy river Ganges.

well, whether that job is menial or grand. This happy, healthy pride is a step in the seeker's development.

While most people seek a spiritual life within the context of life as they live it now, some who come to an ashram find the courage for a greater dedication through sanyas. While visiting the Ramakrishna

Order, I became aware that only twelve years of tapas are necessary. Then the sanyasi can acquire money again because he or she now knows both extremes and can attempt to find a balance between them. Within an ashram, control of the finances rests with the guru, but it is wise, after completion of the period of tapas, for the guru to prepare for financial independence. In this way, when the guru's mind and body begin to fail, the ashram will not suddenly have to assume the burden.

Very often the activities of an ashram diminish after the guru has died, at least until a new leader naturally emerges. In the case of the Ramakrishna Centre, it was ten years before Sarada Devi revitalized it and became a spiritual leader in her own right.

The Western guru might do well to reverse the Indian tradition by allowing initiates to continue living in the ashram. Then the guru can be absent for long periods of time. This allows disciples to unfold their capabilities under the supervision of the initiates. The guru then functions like an ambassador for the ashram, spreading the word to those who are receptive. This can lead to the creation of ashrams in various locations, which is perhaps the most harmonious arrangement, with each ashram having its own autonomy to meet regional needs.

Initiates may also be sent away to start a new center or take charge of another branch of the ashram. It is often at this point that the new leaders begin to appreciate their indebtedness to their own guru. The disciple who has been requested by a guru to start an ashram, either inside or outside the country, is not from the beginning truly a guru. This creates a number of difficulties. Followers who demand to have a self-realized master may pressure the teacher into pretences, or into a silence that is an effort to escape from them.

A new leader, even with the best intentions and utmost sincerity, is bound to blunder in areas in which experience is lacking. The work often seems to be an incredible burden, because he or she does not have the spiritual knowledge of the guru. The new leader may still be wrestling with the concept of the "I" who carries that colossal weight, the "I" who seeks to exercise self-mastery. The development of an ashram reflects the development that "newly-baked" gurus must go through to mature. In this process many flaws will be recognized, and times of depression experienced when lofty ideals cannot be met.

Just as our own personal growth has to be steady and firm with a good foundation of character and quality, so does the growth of an ashram. There is wisdom in slow growth—it is very steady, it is very solid. Things that grow fast are like mushrooms, alive today and gone

The Temple of Light at Yasodhara Ashram symbolizes the essential unity of all religions. Its design is based on a recurring vision of Swami Radha's.

tomorrow. There will always be shaky events in people's lives and there will always be people who do not have the stamina for this way of life. It cannot be helped. But if an ashram as a whole, as an atmosphere, as a base, has a core group that is dependable, then the ashram will continue to grow in a healthy way.

An ashram starts with one individual who puts forward ideas that inspire others and help them to grow. I hope there will be many who do this. To inspire others and to bring out the best in them is a most worthwhile purpose. The ideals that people live by nourish the hope for harmony and peace on earth.

Chapter 23

Finding a Guru

How can you find a reliable guru, a person worthy of that position?

Those who are sincere and want to learn can always find a teacher, even in the form of a cat or dog, an ant or a honeybee. If you can learn through observing any aspect of life and nature, you are also preparing in the best way for surrender to a true guru. Sincerity is your greatest protection.

Seekers can be naive and can rush into a situation on impulse. Thomas Merton describes this in his own life, when he gave away everything he had and then knocked on the door of a monastery, only to be asked if he had anything to contribute. When he admitted what he had done, he was at first bluntly told to go to those to whom he had given everything and be supported by them. But his sincerity was recognized by the Superior and in the end he was accepted, and given exactly the kind of work he had intended to leave. This very human story illustrates the naivete that the seeker may have; but no one can remain naive forever.

Finding the right guru depends very much on the state of the seeker's development. The Indian scriptures say that when the student is ready, the guru appears. But how does the student become ready? By first clarifying with utmost sincerity: Why do I want a guru? What do I hope to receive? An honest evaluation of one's own motivation is the first and the most important step. The sincere seeker will certainly be guided to the right teacher if the desire is to attain knowledge of the Self.

It has been my observation that those who meet with disappointment on the spiritual path have contributed to it themselves through their lack of one or several necessary qualities. It is up to the disciple to develop awareness and intuitive perception, and to cultivate the characteristics of loyalty, humility, and persistence.

When the basic work in self-development has been done, then one can seek the guru through prayer. As Jesus said, "Ask and it shall be given you; seek and ye shall find; knock and it shall be opened unto you."[1] The aspirant should ask for a sincere teacher, making no demands like, "I must have a self-realized guru, and only that." By leaving it to the Divine, then the guru is found and accepted as an answer to one's prayers, which will prevent all disappointments.

We cannot surrender to the wrong person if we live with prayer, but the effort has to be made to discover the power of prayer. Jesus said that if we ask for bread—for what we need—we will receive bread and not stones. Lord Krishna in the Bhagavad Gita says, "I will give you what you ask. If you want me, God, above all, I will become your daily companion."

The seeker's experience seems to depend on what is sought. Because there is good and bad, positive and negative in everyone, each of us chooses on which quality we focus. This was particularly clear to me when I witnessed the two ladies who met Papa Ramdas for the first time: one felt she was in the presence of God, and the other felt she was in the presence of the devil.[2] Any aspirant must decide to what he or she will open—to Divine Light or to dark projections. The choice is always ours.

It would be a mistake for an aspirant to seek a teacher who fits a self-created glamorous image of a guru, rather than a person of superior

---

[1] The Bible, King James Version, Matthew 7:7–11.

[2] See page 60.

Swami Radha in Montreal, posing in front of the tiger skin given to her by Swami Sivananda.

development. The sincerity of the guru shows through his or her lack of pretense, in neither concealing shortcomings nor boasting of scriptural knowledge. A good teacher is one who keeps on learning and puts into practice what he or she teaches.

The desire for excitement, admiration, and self-importance can be gratified by pseudo-gurus of both East and West. The more promises, the more entertainment offered, and the more the guru fits the image of the disciple's dreams, the greater can be the disappointment and the ruder the awakening. Rather than looking for a guru who fits a certain concept, whether that is a spiritual Prince Charming, a wise father figure, or an always-loving mother, aspirants should instead prepare themselves to be receptive and willing to apply self-discipline, assured that through sincere prayer, they will find the guru who will most benefit them.

The need to clarify our goal and purpose of life must be emphasized over and over again. No one can be relieved of this responsibility. Each of us will find what we seek: if we seek the Most High, we will find the Most High. Though our focus we attract others of like quality. Even in daily life we can see this. People who have something in common gravitate together. If a musician moves into another town, very soon he will meet other musicians. When our search for the Divine is single-pointed, then we will be drawn to others of Light. But the Light of knowledge doesn't just descend on us. We have to attract this Light. We have to want this Light so intensely with our total being that we become a magnet, and draw this Light to ourselves.

If the longing for the Most High is sincere and intense, and if maturity is sufficient, aspirants will know that a demanding guru will help them develop more fully and understand more quickly, than will the guru who caters to their weaknesses.

How will you know when you have found your guru? When the disciple meets the guru, they both know, maybe not at the same time and certainly not by mental speculation. But this inner knowing, the knowing of the heart, never deceives. When the disciple has found the guru, he or she will feel uplifted and deeply inspired, and the strength of that inner experience will give life new meaning, purpose, and value.

Chapter 24

Aspirant Illusions

In all Indian texts that deal with the relationship of guru and disciple we find the disciple speaking in superlatives: the precious, the glorious, the one who knows everything from mending pots to being the embodiment of divine wisdom. For the Western aspirant, giving the guru resounding titles such as "Satguru," "Rinpoche," "Gurudeva," or "His Holiness," and thinking of the guru in the Indian way as God manifest, may have some meaning, but may also mislead by encouraging unrealistic expectations. Though gurus may aim for perfection as they see it, we should not expect the personality of the guru in the human body to meet our own concepts of perfection.

I had an opportunity to gain this understanding in my relationship with Swami Sivananda.

He had written in his books that aspirants need to overcome vanity, pride, and the wish to be accepted; and that too much care about external appearance takes energy, and encourages superficiality. I had put in great efforts to overcome my conditioning while in India, since I came from a background where an attractive appearance was highly valued.

On one occasion I talked the other disciples into planning a surprise for Gurudev. We arranged for them to tell Sivananda that a sadhu had arrived at the ashram and wanted to perform Siva's Dance of Bliss for him. For this dance my costume consisted of large, ill-fitting clothes, with a cheetah skin wrapped around my body. I wore a dirty matted wig, my face was smeared with ashes, and I had the three lines of Siva on my forehead. It was not easy to allow myself to be seen looking so unattractive.

During the entire performance Sivananda did not have the slightest idea that behind this disguise was his Western disciple, whom he had recently renamed Radha. When the dance was over he motioned me to him. In order not to give myself away I did not speak but answered him with gestures as if practicing *mauna.*[1] Then I stripped off my wig. He was astounded, but his first remark to me was not a comment on how I had performed the dance. He asked, "Why did you make yourself so ugly?"

I was shattered. This presentation had been intended as a joke and I expected it to be taken that way. When you live with a guru who is supposed to be all-wise and all-knowing, you don't anticipate such a reaction. It was obvious that he was conditioned by hundreds of generations of male ideas about women. My effort to go beyond my needs for emotional security and to give up pleasing others had been no easy matter.

It was some time before I could understand and accept that the preciousness of gurus lies not in their personalities, but in their knowledge. To learn and to apply that knowledge is each disciple's responsibility.

We can read of such discrepancies in accounts of gurus from ancient times. When Guru Marpa's wife handed Milarepa her valuable turquoise, her husband, Marpa, admonished her. However, she pointed out that although everything she had brought to the marriage did indeed belong to him, this gem was hers. It had been given to her by her parents in case she should ever need it, because they knew what a hot-tempered and stingy man he was, for all his saintliness.

Concepts of perfection are in the mind of the aspirant and are influenced by cultural background. The seeker who looks for perfection

---

[1] Mauna is a vow of silence

"I wore a dirty, matted wig, my face was smeared with ashes and I had the three lines of Siva on my forehead. It was not easy to allow myself to be seen looking so unattractive."

in a guru, first must ask, What is perfection? From what view-point? From what background? What appears to be perfect to one person is just barely tolerable to another. The qualities we expect from the guru are the same ones we inflict on God. We tend to create a guru in our minds that we could not find if we searched forever. We must discard these childish ideas and instead consider that we are all travel companions on the same Royal Highway that leads to Higher Consciousness. Some aspirants have a little baggage, some have a lot; some are barefoot, some are on bicycles; some are running, some strolling leisurely. It is the same with gurus, except that they are ahead of us on the journey, pointing the way.

In other words, gurus are also human, which is a point we frequently ignore in assessing spiritual leaders. Even the most highly evolved is limited by the laws that govern the human body and mind. This human aspect can be an inspiration, giving the aspirant some hope of spiritual achievement without having to live up to an impossible ideal of perfection. If gurus were really as perfect as some followers expect them to be, there would be little hope for the imperfect human being who wishes to evolve.

Some aspirants approach a guru with expectations of an instantaneous mystical experience. When I was in India I saw many Western people who arrived, thinking, "I have bought this ticket to India, so now Sivananda has to give me Realization." Because they had bought a ticket they deserved Realization? There was no depth in their thinking.

Some Westerners approach a spiritual teacher with the attitude, "I am gracious enough to come and visit you, now I expect not only a reward, but also proof." That clearly expresses the arrogance of the would-be disciple. My guru had his picture taken with such people, but otherwise gave them no time. He was fully aware that he was criticized by many Westerners, who thought the photographs were his way of seeking publicity. However, Swami Sivananda maintained that this was all he could give to those whose lack of awareness prevented them from receiving more.

On my first visit to India, a Canadian couple who had read my story in the newspaper decided to come to India, too. But because Gurudev wore a coat and glasses, they said, "He's just another businessman," and left. They had a fantasy about the guru. They didn't want to meet a guru, they wanted to meet their fantasy.

Other seekers are seeking emotional gratification: "If the guru asks me to come into his *kutir*[2] every night, gives me a cup of coffee, and

---

[2] A kutir is a cottage.

entertains me with spiritual stories, then I know he loves me." If you want to be gratified on your own terms, then you are not looking at how the guru shows his love and care. For the guru to indulge these wishes would be like a mother who refuses to prepare her child for the challenges of life. The guru has to prepare the seeker for facing the sometimes narrow way to Liberation.

One rather famous American teacher returned from the East saying that he knew his guru was "a great saint" because he had foretold his mother's illness; that was proof enough for him. I wasn't even four years old when, in my childish way, I told my family that my grandmother's sister was going to die, but that didn't mean I was spiritual. Many people have supersensitive perceptions, but these are sensory perceptions nevertheless, and don't necessarily point to spiritual wisdom.

The biggest problem for the Western disciple comes through oversimplification and the tendency to fit everything into pigeonholes. Lack of clarification of one's need for a guru and the inability to accept anything at variance with existing ideas, lead to the greatest self-inflicted pain.

Some aspirants fall in love with the guru. Those who become disciples before they know what it means, before having sufficient preparation, leave themselves open to exploitation. There are gurus who take advantage without shame of those who approach in this way. "If followers don't bother to prepare themselves to receive the teachings and if they don't anticipate the stamina they will need, they deserve to be exploited." I have heard this even from serious gurus.

I remember visiting one male teacher in America. There were four or five women in the room and he mentioned that they had bought his house for him. They were sitting around him, struggling to receive some special attention, some special affection. I told him that I had something to say to these women, but I didn't know if he would want to hear it.

He said, "Swami Radha, you can say anything you want."

So I said to them, "Because you want male companionship, you have chosen him, thinking that you are sexually secure with a spiritual teacher. Everything in your actions says that you are not spiritual seekers, but women who want to win a man. You are not trying to purify your minds, but are battling each other jealously for his attention. You could not convince me that you gave him this house out of great respect for a holy man; you gave it to fill your own needs to be accepted."

Later he confided in me, "I have known that. But that's all they want, so why not let them have it?"

And he had a point. When he started, he did not act in that way. Even a leader who is very sincere in the beginning can become corrupted through the negative responses, the selfishness, and the emotional need and greed of the followers.

People go in search of a teacher. Little do they know what they are looking for. Many women unfortunately look for this kind of spiritual male companionship, and think that the spiritual teacher will protect them from the interference of sexuality. That is not necessarily the case. A male guru has to be a tremendous exception to have overcome the man in him that needs to conquer.

Many Eastern male gurus who have not learned to accept women as equals in their own culture (even though the scriptures may speak a great deal about goddesses), also will not know how to awaken a female Western disciple to awareness and expanded consciousness. If they have a literal interpretation of kundalini as semen rising up to nourish the brain, they simply may not believe that a woman can achieve the kundalini experience.

And many men look for a guru in whom they can reflect themselves. Then they can learn only from another man because they have not yet understood the capacity of a woman, whether she is a yogini or a priestess. Because of the prevalent attitude that men have toward women, they believe that a woman cannot teach them anything of value. So it may take many lifetimes before the aspirant finds the right guru. It is very difficult under ordinary circumstances to find a perfect wife or a perfect husband, but it is much more difficult to find a perfect guru.

Sweet fairy tales of spiritual life are illusions. When the illusion is given an injection of truth, the taste may be bitter, or a little strange and a bit shocking. But for those who are sincere, this truth will also create a great joy—the joy of finding a door open to real spiritual life.

Chapter 25

Pseudo-Gurus

There will always be pretenders who claim sainthood and yet live by double standards, with basic ethics missing from their lives. These pseudo-gurus often have large followings who are attracted by their apparent success. Attracting large numbers of followers is no guarantee of the guru's effectiveness. Quality is not in numbers; there are always only a few who are really sincere.

The argument is often made that everyone worships those who are powerful and successful. But who is "everyone," if not those without awareness? Could any exploiter be successful without complacent people quite happy to be lured and to remain in their ignorance, mistaking it for innocence? Being gullible does not mean being a true seeker; it is only a different kind of gratification and lack of discrimination. If you don't know the difference between a piece of cut glass and a diamond, and you don't care to know, then it really doesn't matter what you are given.

In the West there have appeared a number of gurus from India who have brought the teachings of the East with them. Not all those who have come are among the best, and sometimes the glamor of their orange robes and dark eyes can blind the credulous to their shortcomings. These should not be taken as representative of all gurus or even of the legitimate ones. Saints do not threaten people and saints have nothing to hide.

Many Easterners come to the West "to bring the Great Light," but their real motivation is reputation, is honor, is admiration: "Now I am somebody, not just one of many." Others want only to acquire a permanent visa, wealthy patrons, real estate, and the benefits of Western material life. Still others feel they are justified in playing the role of the guru, even if they are untrained as yogis, because they can supplement their income enough to send money home to their families. There are certain things we would consider dishonest in the West that are not necessarily considered so in the East.

A teacher who did not have correct supervision and guidance when still a disciple will have developed poor working habits and mechanical reactions. A limited ability to concentrate on any discipline or line of thought can lead to giving faulty instructions to followers. Can a guru who displays jealousy and competition toward other spiritual leaders help seekers? Such behavior shows that the personality aspects, each with its own ego, are still in control. Can such a "guru" awaken the Divine in others, if he or she has not experienced such an awakening personally?

Some Eastern teachers who have come to the West interpret the texts to give people what they want. To use the sacred teachings in this way, as an excuse for indulgence in sexual excesses or greed of various types, is an abuse. Disciples need to do what they ought to do, not what they want to do. The fulfillment of personal desires and pleasures is irrelevant. Only a sincere guru will lead them in the right direction.

My teacher, Swami Sivananda, used to say, "If there is a boil and the ointment hasn't worked, in order to make the body healthy again, you have to take a knife and cut the boil out." Of course, who wants to do that? To know that you are creating pain and that some people have a lower pain threshold than others, makes it difficult. But Sivananda's objection would be, "If you would rather see someone lose that hand or arm, then your work is all self-gratification."

There is a saying in scriptural texts, If the guru doesn't do the job because he wants to be liked and accepted and worshipped, both guru and disciple go to hell!

Many great teachers have had disciples who grabbed what they could, claiming it as their own, only to wrap themselves up in pride and self-glorification. Arrogance can lead many aspirants into playing the role of guru themselves, without realizing that this role-playing is more than premature; without the necessary practice, study, and personal experience, it is like the blind leading the blind.

Those whose motivation is self-serving will distort the teachings in the guise of modernizing them. Most aspirants are too naive or lazy to discriminate between distortion and clarification. It is a sad state of affairs that, to meet the needs of the masses, some of the teachings are presented in a perverse manner. To put people into robes and call them sanyasins without training or preparation is as bad as putting a person into a white coat and saying, "You are now a doctor." A change of name and robes does not leave egocentricity behind.

Pseudo-gurus make no attempt to wake people up, but instead lull them further into their fantasies. Most people want a good life, their own satisfaction guaranteed first, and then remember, "Oh yes, there is God also." When a teacher is merely play-acting and is without inspiration, and when self-examination is not required of the disciple, then the basis for a very artificial relationship is established, and a dangerous situation can arise.

Many Western seekers travel to India, and without sufficient experience or knowledge come back to their home country presumptuously calling themselves gurus. They lack discrimination and repeat, more often incorrectly than correctly, what they have heard or think they have heard. Some behave like missionaries; some expound "the only truth"; some appear only once a year to give their *darshan.*[1] Some suffer delusions of grandeur, which many of their disciples share. The fault does not lie solely with the teacher but with the disciple as well, in being attracted to one of similar qualities.

It seems there is an innate desire in human beings of any culture for a power greater than themselves, and somehow to belong to that power or to be in contact with it. This heart's desire is exploited by pseudo-gurus who promise followers special powers by a blessing, a word, a touch. There can be a temporary effect from a touch; something does happen, mainly through the disciple's imagination and self-hypnosis. It is like trimming fruit trees in the spring, bringing the branches inside to an unseasonably warm environment, and watching

[1] To offer darshan is to offer oneself as a focus for the disciple's devotion.

how within a few days, the buds open into tiny flowers. But where is the fruit? There is enough psychic energy in anyone to produce some blossoming, but most of it arises from the emotions and will not bear the fruit of Realization. When the results don't last, the disciples are told they are not pure enough.

Sometimes when an impostor claims to know but misleads and misguides, then the sustaining, creative power of the Divine steps in with a special blessing for the sincere seeker—perhaps through an insightful dream, or through a meeting with someone who can clarify, inspire, or stimulate.

Peace and harmony will never be in the hearts of those who have let the guru down, but neither will the self-professed guru be at peace, who, having stimulated hopes in the minds of disciples, has not shown evidence of those teachings in personal life.

Another problem arises when individuals enter a new field and mistakenly think that they have discovered something original, something that wasn't there before, something of great significance that will turn the world around—not realizing it is they themselves who have "come of age" or are experiencing new perceptions. Rather than accepting the one Light, they see the sun and want to give every ray a different name; or they believe that when the cloud formation is different, the rays are new and exciting, and the old rays are gone.

And so they start a new movement, religion, splinter group, or sect, or they use something from the past to give themselves authority. These people rush in too quickly and thoughtlessly, trying to bring this "new light" to the world. Unfortunately this attitude again shows a lot of ego desire: to be special, to be somebody, to stand out from the masses, to get attention, to be respected, to be admired, and sometimes even to be worshipped.

This need for power becomes very visible in the jealousy and competition of leaders in all religions. Fights, and sometimes even bitter wars among religious movements, should clearly point to the fact that power is being sought. Or does anybody truly think that God, by whatever name and in whatever religion, needs men to defend him, to re-establish his reputation and his honor? Is that not by itself a self-glorification that shatters even the basic idea of what the divine power would be?

Competition, jealousies, and defending one's own perceptions have created many unnecessary problems. Perhaps religion should be declared "dangerous to one's health," when one sees all the fighting, the struggles, the shooting, the injuries, the attacks, generated by people who want to be teachers but have the teachings neither in their minds nor in their hearts. A change of religion has been imposed on many peoples by the threat of the sword or the gun. How can that same religion then claim that God is love? If God is so weak that this divine power cannot reveal itself to the one who is willing to receive humbly and in modesty, then what good is it?

Empty promises given to followers, and the persuasion to remain in the fold of the particular group or religion, are often nothing more than maintaining a certain size of following that will take care of its teachers or priests. Doctrines and regulations are changed for the convenience of those who rule, not necessarily for the benefit of the followers. And so it has gone for centuries and centuries. Competition and self-aggrandizement have left us with a number of religions that have no root except in the minds of those who invented them.

There is an Eastern saying, We can try to understand the sun, but the sun can only reveal itself. We try to interpret the Divine, so the Divine cannot reveal itself to us. Perhaps all these struggles are necessary to help the human being become more mature. Disillusionment may create pain, but it also helps us to grow and to expand our understanding of divine forces. As we expand our understanding, our intelligence, and our consciousness, then old concepts of the Divine die and new ones can emerge.

In yoga we want to go beyond all manifestations of selfishness, to recognize our own divinity. We must discover this divinity within; it cannot be given to anybody. If I am told I have a soul, what does it mean? If I fantasize about an idea that is not born of me, I may never really have contact with the soul. As Jesus said, "The Kingdom of God is within."[2] Let us begin the journey inward, maintaining that particular state of mind that never loses sight of the ultimate reality—the Light.

---

[2] The Bible, King James Version, Luke 17:21.

CHAPTER 26

GURU-DISCIPLE RELATIONSHIP

The relationship between guru and disciple is sacred and needs to be nourished, particularly by the disciple, who then earns the privilege through his or her depth of commitment. When the foundation of the relationship is complete loyalty and absolute honesty, then the karmic effects can indeed be very positive.

Every disciple meets the guru through divine guidance, before any degree of Realization has taken place. At this starting point, the guru is perceived according to the disciple's imagination, ideas, and desires. Some may see the guru as just a bit more advanced, like an older brother or sister, while others are so overtaken by awe and respect that they cannot function. The Westerner also has the old habit of criticism. If disciples insist that the guru meet preconceived ideas from their fantasies, or if they wish to compete with the guru for their ego's satisfaction, then a good relationship is not possible.

The guru is eager to be father, mother, older brother or sister, and best friend all in one. Each day the guru confirms the willingness to share his or her spiritual wealth. Swami Sivananda symbolized this when he distributed prasad—biscuits, oranges, chocolate, or candy—to everyone at the ashram, visibly confirming his care.

The guru knows the subtle signs of a disciple, as a mother knows her child. When seekers come to an ashram, their behavior, actions, approach to people and teachers, all give clues—some very clear and even obvious. If these impressions are favorable and become intensified by the guru's intuitive perception, a mantra initiation might be offered to keep the spiritual inspiration growing.

In the relationship, the disciple's responsibility is to be obedient to the guru, to admit wrongdoings and mistakes, to be straightforward and honest, and never to pretend to agree with the guru when in disagreement. Humility is best cultivated by honesty in communication. Spiritual work and interaction with the guru demand concentration and good mental discipline, as well as openness and receptivity to the inspiration.

The responsibility of the guru is to share knowledge, and inspire students to work toward Higher Consciousness. The guru can teach exercises in concentration that help control the mind, and physical exercises that help maintain the body, but the guru cannot *give* anyone humility, sincerity, or honesty. The guru cannot *bestow* desire for the path of Self-Realization, but can only inspire. The guru cannot force anyone to love God.

Jesus said that some seed falls on fertile ground, some on stony ground. Inspiration will not take root in the disciple if the weeds of self-seeking, self-glorification, and self-importance are left to grow. It is the disciple's work to clear these out. The guru can only plant the seed; the aspirant is the soil, fertile or poor, in which the seed will grow, or the rock on which it will dry out.

After a time, some disciples complain that they have given too much money and unpaid service. But is more likely that they have been overpaid by the instructions they have received, and by the responsibility the guru has assumed for their development. You cannot gain anything without re-giving; without cultivating gratitude, your growth is stunted. The disciple must decide. Traditionally, the guru takes care of the spiritual side and shares knowledge freely and generously. Where could you buy this kind of knowledge for money? Giving to the guru is only the first step in the practice of surrender. Offering something material helps aspirants to discover their attachments, and therefore helps them gain self-knowledge, which is essential for spiritual development.

The best offering you can make to the guru is your total dedication and utmost sincerity.

Disciples often seem a hindrance to the guru. They do not realize the guru's true nature and subject him or her to all kinds of demands and needs. Gurus have to deal with disciples' convictions, immaturity, emotional ups and downs, indulgences arising from instincts and impulses, and desires for an easier way. Some disciples would like to avoid commitment by changing course every six months. Followers who have a tendency toward self-inflicted martyrdom, or those who are possessive and jealous, constantly cause difficulties. Self-importance, desire for personal attention, argumentativeness, mental laziness, and lack of consideration blind them to the needs of the guru.

Although the guru's path is indeed one of independence, he or she also knows that it is through the true disciple that the spiritual work will continue. And so the teacher pressures students to steady their emotional ups and downs, their restlessness and lack of commitment, and encourages them to develop regular practices and honest reflection, so that they can see their own shortcomings and deal with them.

Gurus throughout the ages have always claimed that there were more worthy gurus than deserving disciples. This was Guru Marpa's complaint to Milarepa in the eleventh century, and Longchenpa's[1] complaint in the fourteenth century. Modern gurus are in a predicament because disciples no longer have the necessary powers of concentration and memory, nor the stamina to practice for many hours; so the teachings have to be modified to the disciples' level. But every guru hopes there will be one or two who will want more, to whom the teachings can be truly passed on.

You need fine discrimination to understand the teachings, and to correctly interpret the methods of any guru. The guru who seems to give contradictory instructions might be responding sensitively to the different needs and temperaments of individual disciples. While a very timid person will be encouraged to respond emphatically to a situation, the hot-blooded or ambitious person will be admonished for the same action. You have to observe carefully and try to clarify for yourself what the aim and intentions of the guru might be in different situations. Through your efforts, you can awaken awareness and intuitive perceptions, which are the best possible guides.

---

[1] Longchenpa. *Kindly Bent To Ease Us.* Translated by Herbert Guenther. Oakland: Dharma Press, 1975.

Many Westerners think that disciples become slaves to the master. Not at all. The guru's aim is not to enslave, but to teach disciples to handle freedom perfectly and to become independent. True gurus throw disciples back on their own resources, pointing out the direction and asking students to use their intelligence and power of investigation to find out for themselves. They do not offer answers to puzzling intellectual points or solutions for overcoming difficulties, because they do not want to deprive seekers of the victories that will become a source of strength on the difficult path ahead.

Gurus put their students to the test, not for themselves, but to make disciples realize where they really stand. If a disciple thinks he is already a Vedantist with all powers of the mind fully developed—that he is actually a master, only others cannot see it—the guru will help him to realize what the situation truly is. The guru helps disciples awaken from their illusions.

A guru brings Light into disciples' lives, helping them to see whatever dust and dirt has collected in the basement of their minds. In the beginning every aspirant has little awareness of how much garbage has gathered, and how much Light is needed to destroy the darkness of ignorance, resentment and resistance. The disciple's first task, then, is to discover all of his or her own weaknesses. This is like wiping the dust from the mirror so that the mirror will reflect the Light. Self-importance leads to faulty perceptions and subtle disguises, and sometimes prevents people from investigating the degree of their self-deception. The guru, who may clearly see the disciples' obstacles, guides each toward discovering the inner Self, without going astray.

At times the guru may appear very stern, even cruel, in performing the surgery needed on the disciples' egos. However, true love demands that kind of responsibility. Those who are sincere will understand that the guru is doing what is best for their growth. Some people may feel unjustly criticized by the guru, yet this, too, is part of the learning process that students must be willing to accept. Life, as we all know, often offers unjust criticism. Any tendency to self-justification should be observed.

The guru makes demands on aspirants in order to increase their awareness, as Purushottamananda illustrated by his insistence that his disciples pick up every fallen leaf. When you perceive what is untidy or disorderly on the outer surface, then you can understand something about your own disorderly mind. A disorderly mind is cluttered with lying, pretense, and hypocrisy. Through obeying the guru's demands,

On the banks of the Ganges, Swami Radha meditates with her guru. He wears the cross that she had brought him as a spiritual gift. (The monkey in the background looks on with great interest).

disciples can discover that disorderly mind-states are also reflected in their outward conduct. Someone who lives in a messy, dirty room, but goes out dressed up, clean and tidy, might reflect, "Where do I show off? Where do I pretend by being overly particular? Where is there something untidy that needs to be cleaned up in my life?"

However, for someone who has a tendency to perfectionism and continuous criticism of others, the guru may give just the opposite instructions. Perfectionism is not clarity of mind, but is a result of avoiding criticism under all circumstances. So the guru may encourage such a person to be less painstaking. These disciples are often so busy perfecting for the sake of recognition that they do not really do a good job on themselves. Perfectionism can be an escape from dealing with themselves.

In order to ensure that disciples put their higher values into practice in daily life, a true guru will not only extract work from them, but will extract work for which they will have to carry responsibility. People who wish to run away from life and its responsibilities can be exploited by any self-styled guru who caters to this weakness.

The true disciple surrenders completely to the guru like a baby surrenders to its mother. A baby would not think for a moment, "Will my mother drop me?" Yet it can happen by accident and still the child would not lose faith in the mother. In the same way, in the relationship of guru and disciple a mistake can occur, but still the student should not lose faith in the teacher. How much faith we have is related to how much we pray for faith and strength. The more we are aware that the teacher is the answer to these prayers, the more faith we will have. So of course those who have never prayed for help on their long spiritual journeys, will have more difficulty in having faith in the Divine, the guru, and the Self.

This story from the East captures the sincerity that a disciple needs in the relationship with the guru:

A guru had a lot of people around him who said, "Yes Guruji, yes Guruji."

He soon grew tired of all this so he said, "I will now give everybody a last chance for Realization." He went into his little hut and came out with a huge knife. "If I can cut your head off, then by the courage that you show you will have Realization."

After a long silence one fellow got up and said, "If that is what it takes, then I would rather not have a head."

So the guru took him behind the little hut, motioned him to sit down, then in front of him, killed a chicken. He bloodied his clothes and his knife, and then came back to the rest of the group and asked, "Does anybody else want Realization?" They all left.

Through his courage, his faith in the guru, and his intense desire for liberation at all costs, the willing disciple did achieve Realization.

Developing faith in a person in whom you can see goodness is a steppingstone to developing faith in the invisible, in the Divine. Discrimination is essential. Whenever you see goodness, then happily try to awaken the same goodness in yourself. If you see something that you think is not perfect, then investigate. Weigh the perfections and imperfections, as you see them, against each other.

If you have faith in the Divine already, then you have faith in the spiritual teacher. Your faith carries you. You know that the Divine will not let you down.

Dry periods on the spiritual path are tests of faith. In the guru-disciple relationship, as in all human relationships, we can expect to have faith tested. And when we have met the test, we know that our strength has grown. The disciple's gratitude to the guru—for all he or she is doing, will do in births to come, or has done in previous births—is a quality that when cultivated, becomes a resource in times of spiritual dryness. The guru encourages the disciple not to lose heart, and will continue to prod the disciple until he or she has reached the highest Realization.

The relationship between guru and disciple continues after death even more than in life, because then the soul is freed from the bondage of the flesh. In the physical body, we could not live with a perfect being—we could not breathe, we would continuously be conscious of how mean we still were, how much jealousy, greed, and ego we still possessed—and it would make life unbearable. It is wise, therefore, to develop a close human relationship with the guru and regard him or her as a travel companion who may have had more experiences than you, and can therefore provide advice and assistance to the traveler who enters a new "country."

The Indian scriptures advise willingness to serve the guru. Do anything he or she asks that agrees with your conscience. If you are asked to do something you do not understand or that you cannot accept in good conscience, then discuss it with your guru. Serve the guru. Selfless service makes you divine. Help your guru to serve others. Discard your own desires, because if you take your guru as someone with a greater awareness of the divine presence, then he or she definitely will not say anything that will put you in the wrong spot.

You cannot love God if you cannot love the teacher. No human being can be happy and in harmony without love. Let this love find its expression through surrender, and you will see how love comes from the teacher to you. It will give you awareness, too. If you close yourself up to everything because you want to follow your own ideas, you might as well stay away. This is another kind of selfishness. But if you want to be a servant of God, you become God's servant as a channel of Divine Light. It takes some practice, but with persistence you will succeed.

In the beginning, even the disciple who is very dedicated has no proper understanding of Self-Realization. The aspirant is a spiritual baby unable to assess the guru's creativity in knowledge or language. But a time will come when the devotee moves closer to the guru, learns to listen with the inner ear, searches within, and recognizes the emergence of the inner guru. Then understanding between guru and disciple is at its best.

CHAPTER 27

INITIATION

Mantra initiation is a spiritual marriage between guru and disciple, which cannot be dissolved by the breaking up of the human relationship. Initiation is a privilege, not something to be expected. It is usually given after a relationship of a few years, on the guru's initiative as well as the disciple's request.

The disciple must have seriously reflected upon the implications and must feel assured that in accepting this responsibility, he or she has the persistence and stamina to really pursue the spiritual path. If it is discovered that "I just want a taste of spiritual life—I want to become a little better, a little more honest, and a little more considerate—and that's all I want this lifetime," then it is much better not to seek initiation. Initiation is more intimate and much more binding than even a marriage, because it is a spiritual marriage that lasts until one's own Self-Realization.

The basic question—What is the purpose of my life?—must be posed long before any initiation. The common obstacles—to fight, to be right, to express self-will, to be defensive, to live the way I want, to live by my opinion—must be eradicated, if your goal is spiritual life and Higher Consciousness. Anyone who does not trust in the guru, should not even consider the idea. To be initiated does not mean to belong to a select group of people, or to become a "club member"; that attitude would display an unhealthy pride. People who are very critical of the guru are also better off without initiation, because it will only bring them harm.

Even though the seeker might interpret warnings as rejection, the guru has a responsibility to ensure that those who seek initiation fully understand the depth, demands, and karmic implications of this association, so that the bond will not be formed prematurely.

The disciple should make an effort to clarify what obstacles might be anticipated, and what personality clashes or difficulties could arise. Those that are easy to recognize should be dealt with immediately. Problems in a marriage can often be traced to one partner having a highly idealized image of the other, which in time brings disillusionment and disappointment. Similar problems can develop in this spiritual marriage if the disciple holds a glorified picture of the guru's perfection.

The commitment on the guru's part is to spiritually nourish the initiate, to give whatever he or she has, and if necessary to pursue the disciple over many lifetimes, until the initiate has achieved Liberation. Disciples have to ask themselves what they will give back, not just on the day of initiation, but as a continuous giving. To give one's house, property, or income for the next ten years is no guarantee of commitment. Why should a guru in return take on a responsibility that will keep him or her bound for who knows how many lifetimes?

The following story illustrates the nature of a sincere disciple's offering:

Padmasambhava was an Indian who ventured into Tibet, bringing the ancient teachings. His first students were very poor and simple people. But when the king heard about the power of the teachings, he, too, wanted personal instruction and initiation.

Padmasambhava asked, "What will you give back?"

And the king said, "I will give you many cups of gold, chests of marvellous jewelry, and mountains of riches and treasures."

Padmasambhava said, "No, that is not enough."

The king was amazed. He could not understand it; his offer must have been far richer than that of his poor subjects. How did they get the teachings?

But something in the king wanted the teachings at any cost. So after some deep thought he said, "I will give you my entire kingdom."

Padmasambhava said, "No, that is not enough."

"Not even that?"

He said, "No. Give me what you are most attached to."

And finally the king realized he was most attached to his wife, the source of all his personal pleasures—sexual, emotional, and intellectual. When the king renounced his most precious attachment, he received initiation from Padmasambhava.

Husband, wife, father, mother, brother, sister, education, wealth cannot be put above the guru. The initiate's greatest offering is loyalty, based on a deep trust and confidence. If a disciple says, "I give you my life," then the guru has the right to use that life for the spiritual work. An intellectual understanding of these points is not sufficient; the disciple needs to be dedicated and willing to surrender to the work.

The value of a mantra initiation depends a great deal on the efforts of the disciple in the practice of the mantra. Like a mother who gives birth to a child, the spiritual teacher cannot make the spiritual child grow, but can only contribute to the growth that takes place on its own account—by giving nourishing food, and by keeping the child away from what is hindering and damaging.

The power of money serves as a good example to explain initiation in practical terms. Let us assume that you are given a large sum of money. How you spend it rests entirely with you. You can squander it, you can throw it away, or if you have no understanding of its power, you can bury it in the ground. To make money you have to have money. If money is symbolic of power, consider that initiation provides capital to start your spiritual bank account. The basic power of your sincerity in seeking will generate the interest, and continue to build up the account. The benefit, as stated in the Bhagavad Gita, is the good karma of the disciple, which accumulates and will be available also in another birth.

The promises made at the time of initiation are sacred. Gurudev Sivananda used to tell a story to explain this point:

A devotee who was a merchant had promised his guru a carpet so that those who gathered around to hear the divine wisdom of the guru could sit comfortably, forget their bodies, and become absorbed in his words. But when the merchant reached his own home he forgot all about the promise he had made.

The guru waited patiently for some time, but when he realized that the merchant had forgotten, he called one of his disciples and told him to go to town and remind the merchant of his promise. The disciple was most reluctant to carry out this request. He thought to himself, "The guru preaches the ideal of renunciation to us, and now he not only shows interest in the merchant's gift, but he is actually running after this man to obtain the carpet." But because obedience is one of the first lessons a disciple must learn, he grudgingly walked the several miles into town and at last found the merchant.

When reminded of his promise, the merchant began to loudly lament his forgetfulness. "Because I have kept my guru waiting, I will make amends by sending back with you this very day a carpet that is twice as big and twice as thick as the one I had intended."

And so loaded down with this generous gift, the disciple trudged the long miles back to his guru. As his burden grew heavier, he grew less and less appreciative of the merchant's generosity. By the time he had reached home he was quite furious. He threw the carpet on the floor in front of his guru, and angrily accused him of greed and desires unworthy of a renunciate.

The guru listened to the outburst quietly, nodding his head and smiling at his irate disciple. When the outburst was over he calmly said, "Would you rather have seen our merchant friend suffer because of a broken promise? To break a promise to his wife would not be wise karmically. To break a promise to his friend would also be unwise. But to break a promise to a spiritual person is truly like breaking a promise to the Divine. I knew it would be much kinder to spare our friend any unpleasant repercussions, so I sent you to remind him and to pick up the carpet."

A promise that we give to the Most High, even silently in our own minds, is binding. If we do not fulfill such promises, we incur bad karma, which is why human suffering is endless. We are truly the creators of our own destiny. As the guru points out to his disciple, we must practice awareness in all areas of life, but particularly in regard to the promises we have made.

Some people think they can give an initiation back. According to my guru that is not possible. He would say, "Once you are pregnant, can you say, 'No, I am not pregnant' or, 'Nothing happened, so it is not possible'?" But even if some gurus say they will take vows back, they cannot, because the guru is only a witness to the disciple's promise to the Divine, and it is the guru's duty to help disciples keep their word.

The repercussions of promises made at the time of initiation will reflect in many lifetimes, but they also have their effect in the present.

Swami Radha at the feet of her guru, Swami Sivananda, after her initiation into sanyas. "Initiation is more intimate and much more binding than even a marriage, because it is a spiritual marriage that lasts until one's own Self-Realization."

So there must be mutual trust. The disciple has to trust that the guru will indeed give help and guidance, and share the teachings. The guru has to trust that the disciple will be obedient, loyal, and persevering.

The giving of mass initiations is an Eastern custom intended to help people think of God and to divert their mental activity, to at least a small degree, from the constant scheming to fulfill selfish desires. It is not an initiation in the true sense, but it is a challenge that a few will accept to do something with the mantra. Those who do will finally find their way back to the guru, at which time a new and valid initiation will be given. As in the parable of the sower, the seeds that fall on fertile ground will grow, but those that fall on barren stony ground will die away. The mantra seed, when it is planted in a sincere heart, will eventually flower.

Several initiations from the same guru are only a matter of communicating new instructions. Initiations may be given into different yogic techniques, such as the Divine Light Invocation and Kriya Yoga. The brahmacharya initiation is a vow of celibacy that the initiate makes to the Divine.

To become a sanyasi or swami requires teaching ability, and initiation into sanyas is given by some gurus only when they are sure that the teaching comes from personal experience. Usually the initiation is given after a relationship of six years, but it can also take place sooner or later, at the guru's discretion. It may be given on sudden inspiration, after which a formal initiation will take place, as happened in my own case. Mantra initiation is a necessary step toward sanyas, but is not necessarily an obligation to become a sanyasi.

Sanyas basically means "I renounce this world." Chapter 18 of the Bhagavad Gita describes the path of renunciation, and shows the necessity to renounce mental and emotional fears, and finally to recognize and renounce cherished beliefs. Beliefs have to be tested wherever they grow. To believe that we can surrender, to believe that the Divine will take care of us, does not carry conviction until we have tried it for a sufficient length of time to come to grips with faith. We cannot test faith if we still have $100 in our pockets, if we have a position, or if we qualify for welfare. The sanyasi must renounce personal relationships, and must be exposed to a range of experiences, including total rejection, that will indeed demand stamina.

Renunciation is not easily understood. It means to renounce or to give up attachments. One can be attached to the idea of poverty as well as to the idea of wealth; nor is this true renunciation, but merely a shifting of focus. My guru, Swami Sivananda, showed this principle in an amusing example:

An American came to Sivananda Ashram and smoked one package of cigarettes after the other. Gurudev met him one day and said, "You are still smoking? Still that bad habit of smoking. Ah!"

He said, "Yes, Swamiji, sorry, but I am afraid I can't stop. I don't have enough willpower."

"Oh, it's all right. It's all right." And he called me over and asked, "What is his brand?"

"I think I have seen him smoking such-and-such."

Gurudev gave me some money. "You go to the bazaar and buy a whole box."

So I went, bought a whole box, came back, and Gurudev wrote on a piece of paper that he then stuck on the carton, "You may smoke all these cigarettes in peace, even in bliss. Sit down and do nothing when you smoke but think of Divine Mother. Make yourself a living incense burner!"

This was the incredible ingenuity of Swami Sivananda! The man had smoked because he was so restless; now he did not dare to do otherwise. He sat smoking, doing nothing for whatever time it took to smoke each cigarette.

When Sivananda said I should start ashrams in Canada and America, I asked, "What about people who smoke in the West?"

He said to me, "Make them living incense burners!" And then he added, "One can be just as attached to the idea of non-smoking, as a smoker is attached to the cigarette."

Renunciation is a matter of giving up that attachment.

The acceptance of the initiation and the path is the beginning, but the living and putting it into daily action—and not only daily action but also into daily thinking—is quite a different matter. Mantra initiation is the spiritual marriage in which the indissoluble bond between guru and disciple is formed, making the disciple a link in the chain of gurus who have achieved Realization through the mantra. Sanyas initiation is a spiritual marriage with the Divine, and means putting the ideals of the mantra initiation totally into practice.

Only the person who can recognize the great blessings of the destiny that has brought about a meeting with a true guru, deserves to find such a guide. Be worthy of your spiritual path, the teacher you have found, and the initiation you desire or have received.

CHAPTER *28*

WHAT IS GOD?

During the time that I was in India as a disciple, when I met and talked to various Westerners as well as the gurus I have written about in this book, it became obvious to me that I had to do my own thinking. No answers were given to the problems I turned over and over in my mind. I had to cope with my own questions about God, and because I felt I was in a period of transition, I did not want to come to any premature conclusions. This questioning culminated in the thought, "Why do I want an absolute concept of God? Why do I need such a concept?"

I had difficulty accepting the claim of all scriptures, Western and Eastern, that they are the Word of God. Apparently God had given everyone a different word and I felt that to trust only one would slow my progress rather than set me free. I could not conceive of a Supreme Being who by word of mouth passed on the laws and rules of behavior. The authority given to God in the past seems to have crumbled in any case, particularly in the West, and there seemed little hope that it would survive in the face of increasing education and the development of science. Many of the usual ideas about God as the Absolute, the Infinite, All-Good, All-Merciful, All-Compassionate, the Creator of all and everything, the Eternal, were not acceptable to me, either. Although I did not believe that there is a Supreme Being who dictates the Word, I could accept that saints and prophets of all cultures, because they had less egocentricity and greater understanding, had received revelations that were divine inspirations.

As I looked around and saw what was going on in the world, the concept that God is all-merciful, all-good, and all-compassionate was unacceptable to me. If God created all and everything, then all and everything is God. But everything is obviously not merciful, as demonstrated by man's inhumanity to man. I was greatly bothered to hear of an unmarried young woman who had tried unsuccessfully to abort her child out of fear of rejection. According to the Christian concept that we pay for our sins, what would be the baby's sin? Even the idea of reincarnation did not fully answer this question, but it could at least provide a temporary answer with its concept of past karma, or having chosen the wrong birth channel. But how would a God that is an all-just, all-powerful creator allow this to take place? This all-powerful God seemed not to have assumed responsibility for his creation, otherwise he, being all-knowing, could not have created human beings with so many shortcomings, blind to their own souls or divine spark.

Early in my life I had recognized the impermanence of things, material and emotional, including what is generally called happiness. The many talks that I had with people of all religions were of little help in answering my questions, and yet it was also hard for me to believe that each human being is like an apple on the tree with no purpose at all.

The God that had been presented to me in the little religious education I received in school had given me no meaning or purpose to life. As I repeatedly brought up this point with a variety of people, thinking that perhaps my own understanding fell short, there were always the same gentle, soothing responses: "But why would you look only at this? There are so many other aspects. See what a beautiful world God has created. Look at the flower over there, that marvelous tree, this beautiful child." It seemed to me that people did not want to accept the fierceness and the tough reality—the other side, the shadowy, dark, dramatic side. They liked to believe in a sweet God who provides hope when there is little to hope for.

I saw justice swayed by politics. Man-made law was to me a way of making life more convenient, but I had no respect for it, nor belief in its justice. I saw that the ideas of human law were transferred to God, and there seemed to be a continuous bargaining, pleading, and trying to please God without any solid evidence of success.

These thoughts were very pressing in my mind and heart, and the gurus I met held a great attraction, for they answered questions I had been wrestling with for a long time. They were very important to me, particularly as I slipped at times into moments of depression when everything seemed to be useless, meaningless, and purposeless.

I had been given little encouragement for personal thinking before meeting these gurus, of whom Swami Sivananda was perhaps the most encouraging. The process of questioning all beliefs used by the Tibetan guru resulted in an exhilarating feeling of freedom, although sometimes I felt suspended in midair like a soap bubble that might explode into nothing at any moment.

The practice of yoga, I was told, was to discover my individual consciousness, and from the very beginning the physical aspects of Hatha Yoga gave me the first inkling. I had been unable to accept that God created man in his own image, and considered that perhaps the word *image* had not been precisely translated, or that the meaning had changed over the centuries, or there was something else in me that could be considered the image. So then I thought that perhaps my individual consciousness is that image. And perhaps God is not a Supreme Being, but is Cosmic Consciousness. Then, as an individual endowed with consciousness, I am created in that image.

This thought gave me tremendous joy, and set me free from the painful mental acrobatics that had led me nowhere all these years. With this idea I could accept the good and the bad, the pairs of opposites, and I realized I had a tremendous power when I recognized my freedom of choice. For quite awhile I thought that all my problems were solved, but there were moments when I wondered, "There must be still more. Maybe I am just at the beginning. Maybe I have just put my foot on the first rung of the ladder." However, even that first rung provided a great source of energy.

My peace of mind was occasionally disturbed when I came in contact with Buddhists who told me there is no soul, there is no Self, and that I had not yet discovered my Buddha-nature. This term was never explained satisfactorily and I could not help thinking that for most

Buddhists, except perhaps the truly enlightened, the Buddha took the same place as God for the Christian.

I came to realize that I could not incorporate all schools of thought into my thinking, but I had an intuitive understanding that there would come a point when it would all fit together. I knew that I needed to challenge my own thinking, and grow in courage so that I could place my old concepts in temporary suspension. I had to summon patience and accept the fact that the answers to my questions lay in the future.

It was at Sivananda Ashram that I got at least some intellectual understanding from the Vedantic teachings. I could see that I needed terminology that had personal meaning to me, and it was some time before the translations of Sanskrit terms were helpful. What is called "evil" in Christianity seemed to have no place in Hinduism, although I remembered one Christian priest saying that evil is defined not by God but by man, and that it is nothing more than his incomplete understanding about the perfection of God. But I became aware that Hinduism also demanded an all-powerful deity that needs to be continually appeased and worshipped if we are to have access to the saving grace.

The theory that the guru takes on the karma of the disciple is in the same line of thinking as the idea of "savior" and "sinner." However my observation has been that the guru's help is like a loan of spiritual capital that the disciple will pay back, perhaps by helping with the work of newcomers or spiritual babies, just as older children in a family help with the younger ones. But we cannot repay the loan in full if we have not maintained our loyalty to the one who made the loan to us.

Some Indian gurus seemed a bit too generous in thinking about the help they gave to disciples. I remember one guru asking, after any positive event, "And how does it come about?"

And his disciples would answer in chorus, "By the grace of the guru."

I could not accept this. I felt that if all the growth in a disciple's life was by the grace of the guru, then the path to self-mastery should be painless. But from my own experience, I saw that it was clearly a struggle to undergo changes, and that it required enormous efforts to be free of old habits and patterns.

The gurus that I met confirmed my understanding that as human beings we are indeed masters of our own destiny. Each of us has autonomy and the ability to direct the course of our life by cooperating with the evolution of our consciousness, which is the purpose of life. Each person can only individually experience what is called God or Cosmic Consciousness. No one can really teach another.

Can a father explain to his daughter what it is like to give birth? The mother will be able to explain much better because she has experienced it. But even she can only stimulate thinking. The daughter will know only by having the experience herself. In the same way, any teacher, however great, can only tell us from experience what the path of the Light is. But that is not enough; we have to experience it ourselves to truly know. Understanding or insights can inspire another person, but each of us must do the work of stripping away our own anxiety and need for security, and finally face being alone. The experiences that gurus lead disciples to are nothing more than milestones. At one point there are no more milestones, there is only the awesome knowing that we have to keep going into unknown, imperceptible dimensions.

The guru's inspiration can create a desire, but we are responsible for the intensity of our desire for the Divine, for the intensity of our desire for knowledge. And when we kindle that desire, that love for the Light, then we bring the light of awareness into our minds, and with the help of that inner light, we can make our way back to its Source.

Glossary

Aryavarta An ancient name for India, "Land of the Holy."

Ashram Center created when spiritual seekers, attracted to a guru, gather and live around him or her.

Ashrama The traditional Indian four stages of human life. The first two are given to learning and duty (family, children), the third is learning under the guidance of a guru, and the fourth stage is to become a guru.

Atman The Divine Self in human beings.

Bhagavad Gita (or Gita) A Hindu scripture symbolically depicting the spiritual development of the human being.

Bhajan A song celebrating an aspect of the Divine.

Bhakti The yoga of love; love without a "because" attached to it, without asking anything in return. Also refers to a devotee whose path is worship and love.

Bharata Natyam A south Indian classical dance style.

Bhikkhu A Buddhist monk or mendicant.

Bodhisattva A spiritual teacher who, having attained freedom, chooses to continue to live in order to pass on what has been learned.

Brahmachari A yogic initiate preparing for a life dedicated to spiritual goals by practicing celibacy and renunciation.

Brahmavidya The science of the Absolute or Infinite.

Brahmin A ruling member of the priestly class.

Buddha Buddha means "The Enlightened One." Prince Gautama of India became enlightened and thereby a Buddha. The image of the Buddha is a reminder to pursue the state beyond mind.

Darshan Darshan is being in the presence of someone holy.

Ektar A single-stringed instrument.

Ghat A series of steps going down to the water.

Gopala The name of the child Krishna.

Gopis The maidens who tend the cows. Symbolically the gopis are an extension of Radha, just as a Bodhisattva is an extension of the Buddha. In actual life they are those who consider themselves to be in the service of the Most High.

Guha Hindi word for cave.

GURU *Gu* means "darkness," and *ru,* "the dispeller." As the dispeller of the darkness of ignorance, the spiritual teacher is called guru.

GURUDEVA The guru, as a symbol of the Divine, is called Gurudeva by disciples.

KALI Divine Power symbolized in the form of a woman who gives birth to one child while she devours another. The message is that life is birth and death; both have to be accepted.

KAMANDALU A water container used by yogis during their spiritual practices.

KARMA The law of cause and effect, often understood only as a law of punishment and reward. Karma is also interaction and interpenetration, and provides the challenges needed for one's own evolution and development.

KSHETRA A place for pilgrims to stop on their way to Mt. Kailas, the holy mountain in the Himalayas.

KUNDALINI YOGA A path of conscious cooperation with one's evolution described in an ancient symbolic picture language. Daily experience of the senses, mind, and energy is explored and refined through spiritual practises.

KUTIR Cottage.

MALA A string of 108 beads used in reciting one of the names of the Divine.

MANTRA A combination of sacred syllables that forms a nucleus of spiritual energy, and is chanted to achieve single-pointedness of mind.

MAUNA A vow of silence.

MAYA Illusion. Mind is creative, producing illusions it believes to be reality. Attachment to these illusions is the source of our pain.

NAGA A mendicant who, at a certain stage, wears no clothing, having achieved control over sexual stimulation.

NAMASTE The reverent Indian greeting in which the hands are placed together at the heart center, symbolizing "The Divine in me salutes the Divine in you."

OM NAMAH SIVAYA Mantra invoking the power of Lord Siva.

PARVATI Consort of Lord Siva. Her name means "Daughter of the Himalayas."

PRANA A very subtle energy travelling with the breath just as a flower's fragrance travels through the air. Prana can be stored in the body.

PRANAM A salutation of respect and devotion.

PRANAVA The cosmic sound heard in the right ear with certain practices, and sounds like a wave of the ocean.

PRASAD Food offered by the guru to the disciple, symbolizing the promise to share spiritual teachings.

PUJA Worship of the Divine by ritual, song, prayer, and meditation.

RADHA AND KRISHNA Radha is the Mother of the Universe, and as a mother loves her child, so does Radha love her creation. Therefore, *Radha* means "Cosmic Love." *Krishna* means "The Black or Dark One," because we can never know all of the Divine. Radha and Krishna are a unit, symbolizing Divine Power manifesting.

RAGA (male) and RAGINI (female) are melodies in Indian music that are governed by precise rules.

RAM The king of the Ramayana, the symbolic story of mankind.

RINPOCHE A title of respect for a Buddhist teacher. The name means "The Precious One."

RISHI A seer, visionary, or spiritual individual of great sensitivity. Rishis were poets of the ancient teachings.

SADHU A wandering mendicant, a holy man living a spiritual life independent of any institution, following a path he has laid out for himself.

SAMADHI Samadhi is experienced in deep meditation, a return to Oneness. Can also refer to a burial place.

SAMSKARAS The impressions of past thoughts and actions, which influence present and future thoughts and actions.

SANGITA Man-made music; as contrasted with unstruck sound, the cosmic Aum.

SANYAS The renunciation of action based on desire. It also refers to a formal initiation of a disciple into a life of selfless service.

SANYASI OR SANYASINI A renunciate whose life is devoted to the service of humanity.

SATSANG A time when seekers gather to chant, pray, meditate and worship. It means "the company of the wise."

SHANKARACHARYA One of four spiritual leaders for each corner of India, of similar authority to the pope within the Roman Catholic Church.

SITAR An Indian stringed instrument.

SIVA A personification of Cosmic Energy, the source of creation.

SIVALINGA Symbol of continuous creation, the promise that human life will continue.

STUPA Sacred mound or monument housing Buddhist relics.

SUTRA Aphorism that encapsulates a doctrine.

TAMPURA An Indian stringed instrument used as a background drone.

TAPAS A concentrated discipline and austerity; a burning, flaming devotion to attaining the spiritual goal.

TANKA A Buddhist wall hanging used for prayer and meditation.

TONGA A horse and buggy taxi.

VEDANTIN A follower of Vedanta (school of Hindu thought based on the Upanishads, a philosophical treatise concerning the origin and potential of humanity).

VIPASSANA A Buddhist system of meditation based on observing the mind.

VISHNU The preserving aspect of the Divine.

WHITE TARA A Tibetan Buddhist form of Divine Mother, the Bodhisattva of Compassion.

YOGI OR YOGINI A person who seeks or attains Oneness or Divine Union.

INDEX